MAX WAINEWRIGHT

DESIGN ANIMATE AND CREATE

WITH COMPUTER GRAPHICS

QED

Quarto is the authority on a wide range of topics.

Quarto educates, entertains and enriches the lives of our readers—enthusiasts and lovers of hands-on living.

www.quartoknows.com

Editor: Claudia Martin
Design and illustration: Dan Newman

First published in the UK in 2017 by QED Publishing
Part of The Quarto Group
The Old Brewery, 6 Blundell Street, London, N7 9BH

A catalogue record for this book is available from the British Library.

ISBN 978 1 78493 746 1

Printed in China

Microsoft Paint is a component of Microsoft Windows developed by the Microsoft Corporation.
See https://www.microsoft.com

OpenOffice Draw is a component of Apache OpenOffice developed by the Apache Software Foundation.
See http://www.openoffice.org

Scratch is developed by the Lifelong Kindergarten Group at MIT Media Lab.
See http://scratch.mit.edu

SketchUp is developed by Trimble Inc.
See http://www.sketchup.com

Internet safety

Children should be supervised when using the internet, particularly when using an unfamiliar website for the first time.

The publishers and author cannot be held responsible for the content of the websites referred to in this book.

Picture credits

4tl Tourbillon; **4tcr** Shutterstock/Marc Dietrich; **4cl** Shutterstock/ChuckChee; **4bcr** Shutterstock/Diversepixel; **4bl** Shutterstock/Marylia; **8cl** © ADAGP, Paris and DACS, London 2016; Private Collection/Photo © Christie's Images/Bridgeman Images; **8cc** © DACS 2016; The Sherwin Collection, Leeds, UK/Bridgeman Images; **8cr** Piet Mondrian [Public domain], via Wikimedia Commons; **12c** Dreamstime/Marish; **20cb** Shutterstock/Gormaymax; **22cl** © The Josef and Anni Albers Foundation/VG Bild-Kunst, Bonn and DACS, London 2016; Private Collection/ © The Joseph and Anni Albers Foundation/Photo © Christie's Images/Bridgeman Images; **22cc** Kazimir Malevich; Getty Images/Universal Images Group; **22cr** Getty Images/DeAgostini; **28cl, cr** Shutterstock/Rawpixel.com; **28ccl** Shutterstock/Sandratsky Dmitriy; **28ccr** Shutterstock/Stock Studio; **28bc** Shutterstock/Andrey Arkusha; **32br** Shutterstock/Michel Borges; **33cr, blb** Shutterstock/Samuel Borges Photography; **33br** Shutterstock/Nolte Lourens; **33blt** Shutterstock/Monkey Business Images; **33blcb** Shutterstock/bikeriderlondon; **34bl** Shutterstock/Piotr Krzeslak; **35br** NASA; **36cr** Shutterstock/Alina R; **36tl** Shutterstock/Marafona; **40cr** NASA; **42tr** Shutterstock/Johnny Adolphson; **42br** Gregory H. Revera; **44cl** (boy) Shutterstock/Cherry-Merry (background) Shutterstock/3841128876; **44cr** Shutterstock/Sahachatz; **46cr** Shutterstock/Monkey Business Images; **46cll** Shutterstock/Photomaxx; **46clc** Shutterstock/ARTdeeva; **46clr** Shutterstock/Shalunts; **50cl** © ADAGP, Paris and DACS, London 2016; urbanbuzz/Shutterstock.com; **50c** Banksy, London, 2006; BMCL/Shutterstock.com; **50bl** Shutterstock/dalli; **51tl** Dreamstime/Yael Weiss; **70cl** Frank Lloyd Wright/Aline Barnsdall Complex; Shutterstock/TrekandShoot; **70c** William Lescaze; Shutterstock/Ron Ellis; **70cr** Centre Le Corbusier; Shutterstock/Philip Pilosian.

CONTENTS

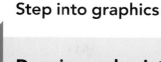

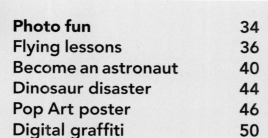

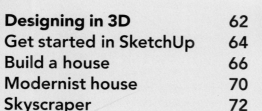

STEP INTO GRAPHICS

The first Bulgarian computer: 'Vitosha', 1963.

A bit of history

The first computers were very different from the laptops, tablets and PCs we use today. As well as being much bigger and slower, they could only display very basic information – just the results of simple calculations.

At first, screens were one colour. They showed 'bumpy' green text on a black background.

As technology developed, keyboards and screens became the standard way to communicate with computers.

By the 1980s, graphics were in colour – and things began to get exciting. People could buy home computers and play games on them. Software developers designed software that let anyone make pictures out of pixels, or dots, of colour.

New technology meant graphics got better and better. Cameras started to use computers instead of film to store photos. Movie companies used computer graphics more and more. In 1995, *Toy Story* was the first full-length computer-animated film. Today, it is hard to see what is real and what is a CGI, a computer-generated image.

Nowadays we are used to seeing high-quality pictures, photos and video on computers, phones and even watches. But how are those images created? This book will teach you how to become an expert at computer graphics.

What you will learn

We will start by using painting programs to make **bitmap graphics**. Bitmaps are made up of a grid of pixels of different colours. Many of the images you see on the web, as well as illustrations in books or on products you buy, are created using bitmap graphics.

Welcome to Max's room

We'll take our skills to the next level using **vector graphics** programs. These create images out of collections of shapes. Vector graphics are often used for creating logos and product packaging.

We will move on to **photo-editing** techniques used by professional photographers and designers. If you look around, you'll see these techniques everywhere, in adverts, magazines, newspapers and even art galleries.

AAAARRGH!

If you fancy yourself as a film-maker or video game-developer, we'll dip into **animation** and how to add animations to computer games.

Finally, we'll enter the world of **3D graphics** to create buildings and even a city. 3D graphics are used by engineers, architects, product designers, game-developers and film-makers.

What will you do first?

1 DRAWING AND PAINTING

This chapter will show you how to master bitmap painting. In this type of art, the pictures you create are stored in a 'bitmap', which is a special kind of grid made up of picture elements, or 'pixels'. Most computers use a grid of at least 1024 x 768 pixels, but many advanced ones use four or five times that number.

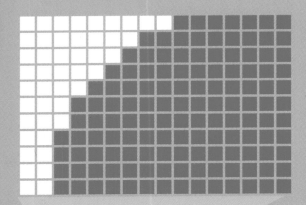

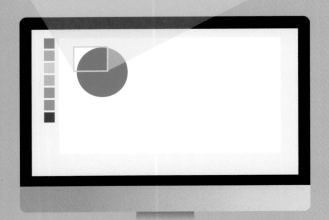

What software can I use?

You can use many programs to try bitmap painting. In this chapter, we will focus on **Microsoft Paint**. This is a free program that will already be on your computer if it is a PC or laptop that runs Windows. If you are using a Mac computer, try a free program called **Paint X Lite**, which is similar to Microsoft Paint. For more information on painting software, turn to page 76.

Common tools used in bitmap painting software

Brush
For simple painting.

Line
For drawing straight lines.

Ellipse
For drawing ovals.
(Hold **'Shift'** down for circles.)

Rectangle
For drawing rectangles.
(Hold **'Shift'** down for squares.)

Rounded rectangle
For drawing rectangles with round corners.

Fill
To quickly colour in a shape.

Text
To add writing.

Rubber
To remove part of your painting.

Line thickness
To choose how thick a line or the edge of a shape will be.

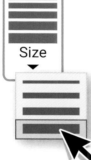

Size

Colour palette
To choose a colour.

Pipette
To pick the exact colour by clicking on part of the picture.

Colour editor
To use numbers or sliders to set a colour of your own.

Top tips for being a great bitmap artist

Use Undo
When you make a mistake, don't use the rubber! It can often make things worse. Just click **Undo**! (A shortcut is to hold down **'Control'** and tap **'Z'**. On a Mac, hold **'Cmd'** and tap **'Z'**.)

Zoom in, zoom out
If you need to draw something small, zoom in using the **Magnifier** or the **Slider**. If you need to get an overview of your picture, zoom out. In **Paint X Lite**, use the **View** tab or menu to zoom.

Be selective
Use the **Select** tool to choose parts of your pictures to move, resize or delete. You can also use it with the tools below.

Be a copycat
If you have drawn one eye and need another, copy the first one using this tool.

Paste
After you've copied something, you need to paste it down. Remember, **Copy** and **Paste** always stick together!

Rotate and Flip
Use the **Rotate** and **Flip** tools to turn or to create a mirror image of a shape.

WALL ART

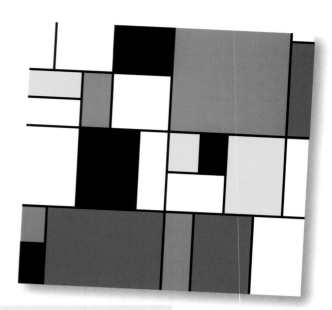

We're going to start by making a picture inspired by De Stijl ('The Style'). This was a 20th-century Dutch art movement that made use of vertical and horizontal lines, with primary colours plus black and white. Any painting software will let you draw straight lines, and fill with colour. With a couple of extra techniques, you can make a piece of art to hang on your wall.

1 Start by looking at some examples of De Stijl art. Ask an adult if you can use the Internet, then search for **'mondrian'** or **'de stijl paintings'**. Click **'Images'**. Here are some examples of things you might find:

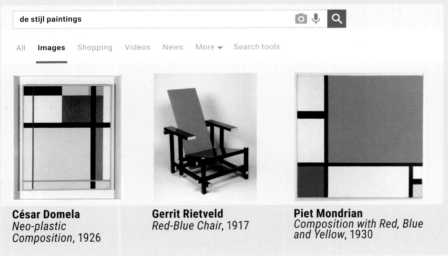

| de stijl paintings | |

All **Images** Shopping Videos News More ▾ Search tools

César Domela
Neo-plastic Composition, 1926

Gerrit Rietveld
Red-Blue Chair, 1917

Piet Mondrian
Composition with Red, Blue and Yellow, 1930

2 Start up your painting program. We are going to use **Microsoft Paint**, but you could use other software (see page 6).

3 Choose the **Line** tool.

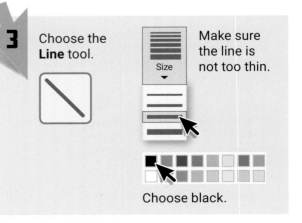

Make sure the line is not too thin.

Choose black.

4 Start drawing horizontal lines.

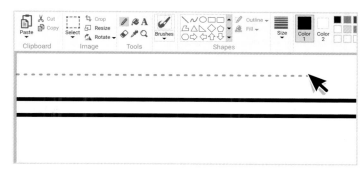

TIP: Hold down the **'Shift'** key while you drag to make sure your lines are horizontal, vertical or at 45 degrees.

---

5 Now draw some vertical lines.

Add some more horizontal lines if you want to.

Remember to hold down the **'Shift'** key.

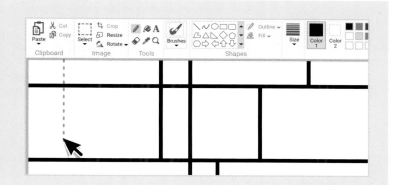

---

6 Choose the **Fill** tool.

Choose a colour.

Click inside the rectangles to start filling in parts of your picture.

TIP: Click **Undo** if you make a mistake. Then try again!

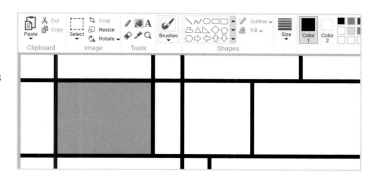

Explore and experiment

Experiment with the techniques you have learnt so far. To make your picture in the De Stijl style, use a limited range of primary colours, plus black and white. Or go your own way, like we have.

Remember to save your work every few minutes.

Print your work when you have finished. Then display it proudly on your wall!

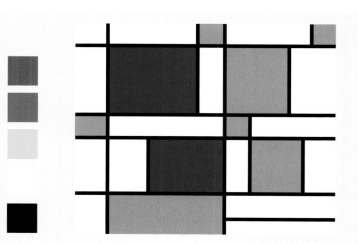

SPOTTY WRAPPING PAPER

In this activity, we will make colourful, dotty wrapping paper. To draw lots of circles quickly, we'll be using Copy and Paste. This will make sure that all the circles are the same size. When you've finished, print out your artwork and use it to make your presents look fantastic.

1 Start by looking at how other artists work with spots. Ask an adult if you can use the Internet, then search for **'coloured spots'**. Click **'Images'**. Here are some examples of things you might find:

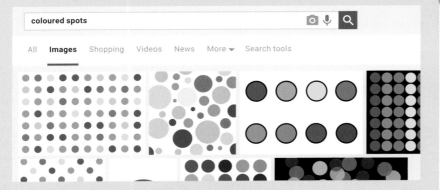

Spot the artist

Some famous artists have made spot paintings. The English artist Damien Hirst has made over 1,000 of them.

2 Launch your painting program.

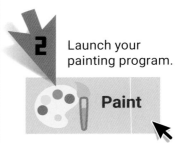

Paint

3 Click the **Ellipse** tool and draw a small circle in the top left corner of the page.

Hold down the **'Shift'** key while you draw to make sure it is an exact circle, not an oval.

Click **Undo** if you make a mistake. Then try again!

4 Choose the **Fill** tool. Click inside the circle to colour it in.

5 We need to make another circle exactly the same size.

Click the **Select** tool.

Draw a dotted line around the circle.

Click **Copy**.

Click **Paste**.

Drag the new circle next to the first one. Carefully make sure they line up.

---

6 Now copy the two circles together.

Click **Copy**.

Click **Paste**.

Click the **Select** tool.

Draw a dotted line around both circles.

Drag the two new circles next to the first two. Make sure they line up.

Now repeat this step with all four circles until you have a whole row of circles.

---

7 Choose the **Fill** tool and work along the row, colouring the circles.

---

8 Choose the **Select** tool again and copy the whole row.

Click **Copy**.   Click **Paste**.

Carefully drag the new row into place beneath the first row.

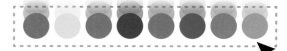

Now repeat this step with both rows until you have a whole screen of circles. Recolour them if you wish.

Save and print your work. Why not display it on the wall, or use it as wrapping paper for gifts or to cover your diary?

11

ROBOT DOOR HANGER

To practise doing some trickier drawing, we are going to make a robot picture. We'll look at how to use shapes to create different parts of the robot. By using Copy and Paste we'll duplicate the robot's arms and legs. Finally, you can print out the robot and hang him or her on your door with a message.

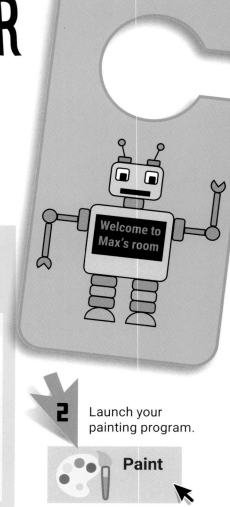

1 Start by looking at some robot pictures. If you have a robot book, you could use it for ideas. Otherwise, ask an adult if you can use the Internet, then search for **'robot clipart'**. Click **'Images'**. Here are some examples of what you might find:

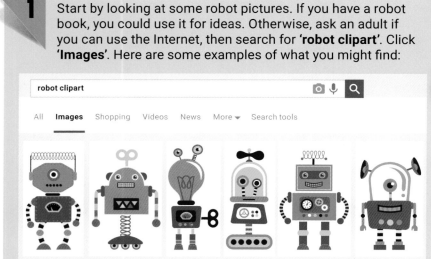

2 Launch your painting program.

Paint

3 Choose the **Rounded rectangle** tool.

Draw three rounded rectangles: one for the head, one for the neck and one for the body.

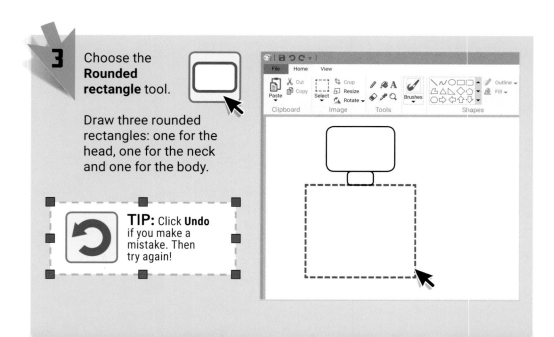

TIP: Click **Undo** if you make a mistake. Then try again!

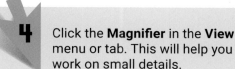

4 Click the **Magnifier** in the **View** menu or tab. This will help you work on small details.

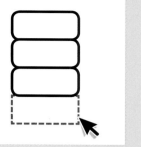

Draw four or five rounded rectangles to make the sections of the robot's leg. We will just draw one leg and foot to begin with, then we will copy it in Step 9.

You may need to click the **Rounded rectangle** tool again after each section.

5 Zoom out to 100% so you can see how your picture is looking.

Now use the **Magnifier** (on the **View** tab) or **Slider** to zoom in again. Keep using this process to help you zoom in and out on detail.

6 Click the **Ellipse** tool and draw a rough circle below the leg to make the robot's foot.

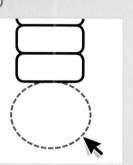

7 Click the **Select** tool. Draw a dotted rectangle around the bottom half of the foot.

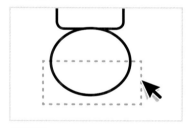

 Press the **'Delete'** key on your keyboard.

8 Click the **Line** tool. Draw a line to make a flat bottom for the foot.

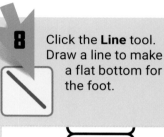

Explore and experiment

Why not give your robot special springy sections on their feet or in their knees?

 Maybe they need different feet that allow them to grip on to things?

 1 Zoom in to work on small details like these.

 2 Use the **Line** tool to draw part of the foot.

 3 Use the **Select** tool to draw a dotted line around a couple of toes.

 4 Use **Copy** and **Paste** to make more toes and drag into place.

13

9

Now we will duplicate the leg.

Click the **Select** tool.

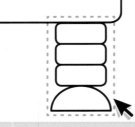

Draw a dotted line right around the leg.

Click **Copy**.

Click **Paste**.

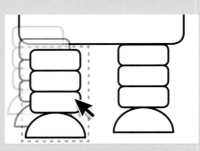

Drag the new leg into place.

10

Our robot needs some arms.

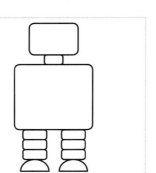

Zoom in then use the **Rounded rectangle** and **Ellipse** tools to draw one arm:

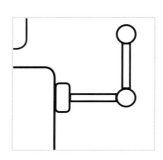

Use the **Rubber** to rub out part of its hand...

...then the **Line** tool to make it into a grabber.

11

Now we will duplicate the arm.

Click the **Select** tool and draw a dotted line around the arm the way we did in step 9.

Click **Copy**.

Click **Paste**.

Click **Rotate** then **Rotate 180°** to make the arm the other way round.

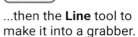

| Rotate ▾ |
| Rotate right 90° |
| Rotate left 90° |
| Rotate 180° |

Then drag it into place.

12

Zoom in and draw the face using shapes. **Copy** and **Paste** the features.

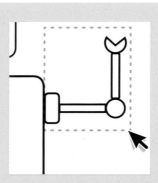
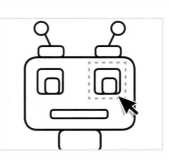

13 Use the **Fill** tool to colour in your robot. See page 6 for help.

TIP: Make sure there are no gaps in your shapes when you fill them in . . .

. . . or the colour will leak out of the shape. If that happens, click **Undo**.

Fix the gap with the **Line** tool or the **Brush** and try filling the shape again.

14 Draw a **Rectangle** to make a screen on the robot.

Use the **Text** tool to type a welcome message.

Welcome to Max's room

 Print out your robot.

 Cut it out.

Stick your robot on your coloured card door hanger.

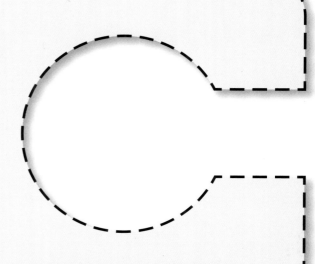

Use this shape to make a template for your door hanger.

Put a piece of paper over this page and trace around the shape. Cut it out and lay it on a piece of coloured card. Draw round your template and cut out the shape in card.

ROMAN INVASION

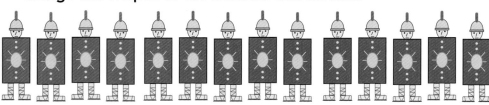

Now you're going to learn how to draw and paint a Roman centurion. We'll use shapes and parts of shapes to create the centurion, zooming in and out to add detail. Finally, we'll use Copy and Paste and resizing techniques to create a whole army. This is perfect if your history topic is Romans! But you can use the same skills to create an army of Vikings or pirates, too. You will just need to change the shapes of the helmets and shields.

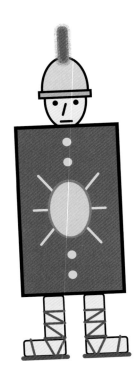

1 Start up your painting program.

Paint

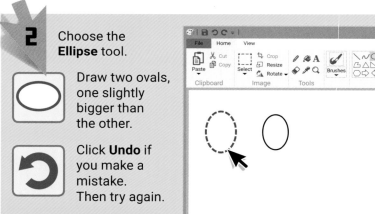

2 Choose the **Ellipse** tool.

Draw two ovals, one slightly bigger than the other.

Click **Undo** if you make a mistake. Then try again.

3 Click the **Select** tool. Draw a dotted rectangle around the bottom half of the big oval.

Press the '**Delete**' key on your keyboard.

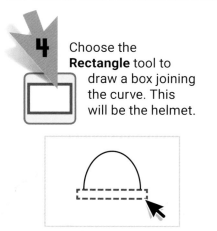

4 Choose the **Rectangle** tool to draw a box joining the curve. This will be the helmet.

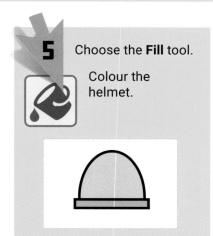

5 Choose the **Fill** tool.

Colour the helmet.

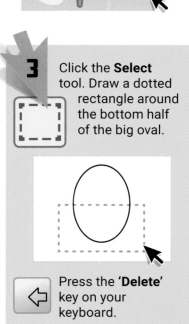

6 Click **Brushes**.

Choose **Spray**.

Size

Set the size.

Spray the feathered plume using red.

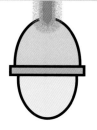

TIP: If you can't find the colour you want...

...click **Edit colours** and set your own.

There are over 16 million to choose from!

7 Click the **Select** tool. Draw a dotted rectangle around the helmet.

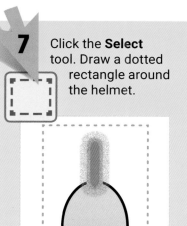

8 Drag the helmet over the other oval.

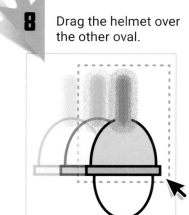

9 Choose a colour for the face.

Choose the **Fill** tool.

If the colour 'leaks' outside the face, click **Undo**. Zoom in to look for any gaps in your lines. Fix them with the **Brush** tool.

10 Now we will draw the face. Click the **Magnifier** (on the **View** menu or tab) to zoom in.

Choose the **Brush** or **Line** tool and draw a face for your centurion. Zoom in further if you need to.

Now zoom back to 100%.

100% ⊖ ━━━▮━━━ ⊕

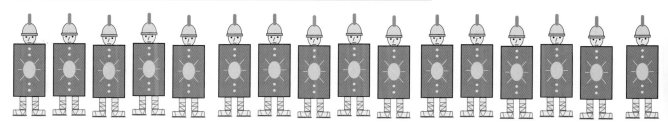

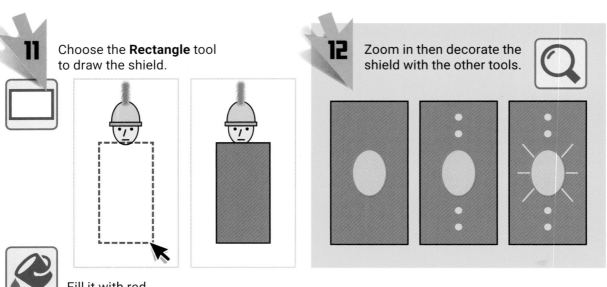

11 Choose the **Rectangle** tool to draw the shield.

Fill it with red.

12 Zoom in then decorate the shield with the other tools.

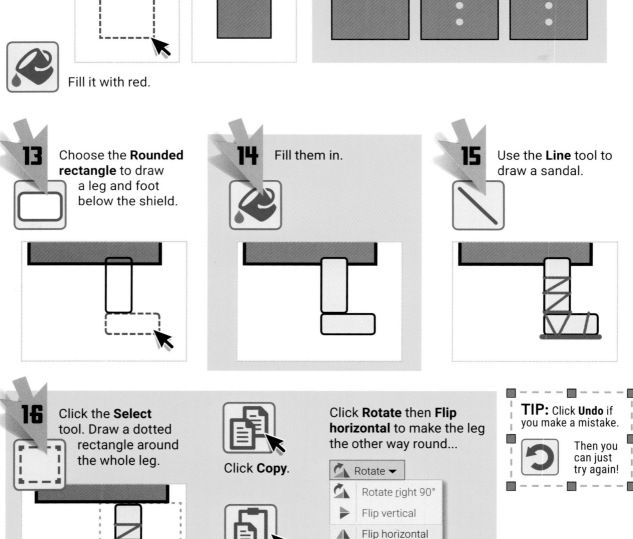

13 Choose the **Rounded rectangle** to draw a leg and foot below the shield.

14 Fill them in.

15 Use the **Line** tool to draw a sandal.

16 Click the **Select** tool. Draw a dotted rectangle around the whole leg.

Click **Copy**.

Click **Paste**.

Click **Rotate** then **Flip horizontal** to make the leg the other way round...

Rotate ▾
Rotate right 90°
Flip vertical
Flip horizontal

...and drag it into place next to the other foot.

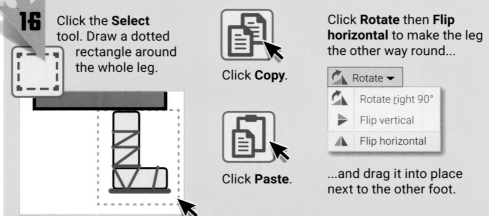

TIP: Click **Undo** if you make a mistake.

Then you can just try again!

17

Using the **Select** tool, draw a dotted line around the whole Roman centurion.

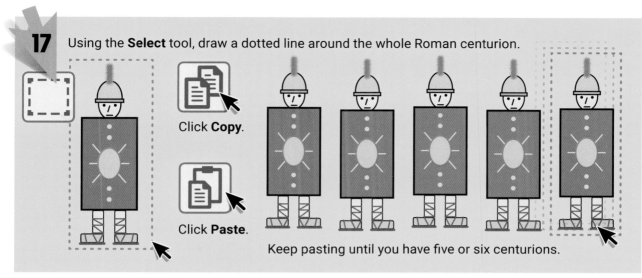

Click **Copy**.

Click **Paste**.

Keep pasting until you have five or six centurions.

18

Draw a dotted line around the whole row. Drag the corner inward to shrink them.

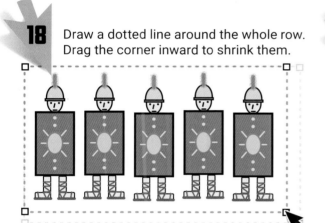

19

Now copy the group of shrunken centurions.

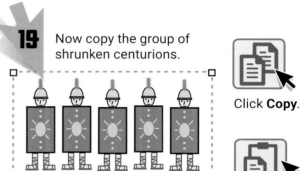

Click **Copy**.

Click **Paste**.

Drag the new group to line them up next to the first group.

20

Keep pasting until you have a whole row of centurions. You can shrink them all again if you need to – see step 18. Copy the whole row and paste again...

...until you have a whole legion!

Explore and experiment

Draw a Viking raider instead:

Make a Viking shield from circles and lines.

To make a Viking helmet, start with steps 2 to 5.

Then see if you can follow these steps to complete the helmet.

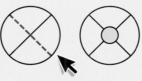

2 VECTOR GRAPHICS

In this chapter, we will do five amazing projects using vector graphics. Rather than treating a picture as a grid of pixels, vector graphics programs treat a picture as a collection of objects or shapes. You can choose the colour, size, position and angle of each object. If you think of a bitmap as being similar to drawing with coloured pencils, vector graphics are more like making a collage.

What software can I use?

The program we are going to use is **OpenOffice Draw**. It is part of the Apache OpenOffice suite of free software. It will work on a PC, Mac or Linux computer. Other programs, like **Microsoft Publisher** and **Adobe Illustrator**, also work with vector graphics. For information on downloading OpenOffice, turn to page 76.

Bitmaps versus vector graphics

Bitmap

Hard to change
Although you can use the **Undo** button and the **Rubber** tool, it is hard to change just part of a bitmap picture.

Quality can be 'bumpy'
When you print out a bitmap artwork, you can usually see bumpy parts and jagged lines, especially when you use circles or make your pictures big.

Edit each pixel
You can edit the individual pixels within a photograph.

More memory
It takes up more memory to store a bitmap graphics image.

Vector

Each shape is separate
You can edit each shape when using vector graphics. You can move it, recolour it, resize it or rotate it.

Picture quality is smooth
You can resize a vector graphic and it will always look smooth.

Only edit the whole object
You can paste a photo into a vector graphics program, but you will only be able to do things to the whole photo.

Less memory
Vector graphics don't take up so much memory. This means you can store more of them on a computer, and download or share them by email more quickly.

Common tools used in vector graphics programs

Shape tools
To add various shapes to the page.

Line tools
To add straight lines or lines with arrowheads.

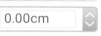

Line style
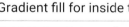
To choose solid, dotted or dashed lines.

Line width
To choose the width of your lines in centimetres (cm).

`0.00cm`

Line colour
`Grey`
To choose the colour of the shape's border.

Area style
To set solid colour or Gradient fill for inside the shape.

`Colour`

Area colour
`Blue`
To choose the colour inside the shape.

Undo
Clicking **Undo** is the best way to handle mistakes.

Zoom
Use the zoom control to get a better view of what you are working on.

Select
Choose this, then click a shape you have drawn. You can change its colour, size, angle and position, or delete it.

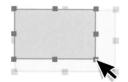

When a shape is selected, green handles will appear. Drag the green handles to resize the shape.

If you click the shape again, the handles turn red. Drag the red handles to rotate the shape.

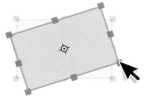

Back to front

Unlike in bitmap painting, all objects are placed on top of each other in a stack. Draw a few shapes then experiment:

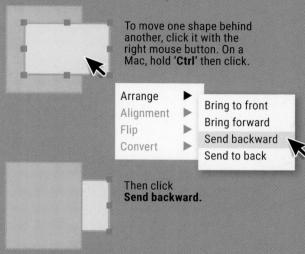

To move one shape behind another, click it with the right mouse button. On a Mac, hold '**Ctrl**' then click.

Arrange ▶	Bring to front
Alignment ▶	Bring forward
Flip ▶	Send backward
Convert ▶	Send to back

Then click **Send backward.**

Copy and paste

Once you have selected a shape, use the **Edit** menu to copy and paste it or duplicate it. To delete a shape that has been selected, press the '**Delete**' key (on a PC) or '**Backspace**' (on a Mac).

To duplicate a shape, click it to select it.

Edit
Undo
Restore
Cut
Copy
Paste

Click the **Edit** menu then **Copy**.

Edit
Undo
Restore
Cut
Copy
Paste

Click the **Edit** menu then **Paste**.

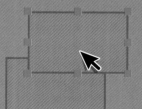

The duplicate shape will appear on top of the original shape, so drag it away to see both shapes.

GET ABSTRACT

We'll get started with vector graphics by exploring shape-based art, learning to move and colour rectangles and squares. Many famous artists have created abstract paintings made up of different coloured shapes. This style of painting is often called geometric abstract art.

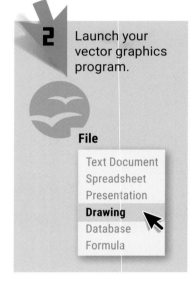

1 Start by looking at some examples of how other artists work with shapes. Ask an adult if you can use the Internet, then search for **'geometric abstract art'**. Click **'Images'**. Here are some examples of things you might find:

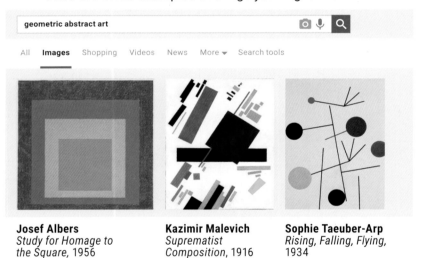

geometric abstract art

All **Images** Shopping Videos News More ▼ Search tools

Josef Albers
Study for Homage to the Square, 1956

Kazimir Malevich
Suprematist Composition, 1916

Sophie Taeuber-Arp
Rising, Falling, Flying, 1934

2 Launch your vector graphics program.

File

Text Document
Spreadsheet
Presentation
Drawing
Database
Formula

3 Find the **Drawing** toolbar. Click the **Rectangle** tool.

Draw a few rectangles by dragging with the mouse. You may need to click the **Rectangle** tool again for each shape.

Hold down the **'Shift'** key while you drag to make perfect squares.

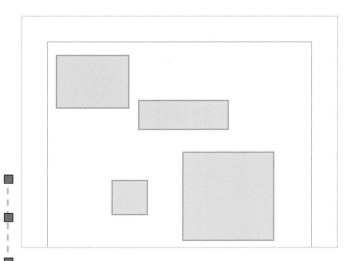

TIP: If you can't find the **Drawing** toolbar, click the **View** menu, then **Toolbars**. Tick **Drawing**.

If you can't find the **Colour** drop-down menu in step 5, click the **View** menu, then **Toolbars** and **Line and filling**.

4 Click on one of the rectangles you have drawn to select it.

Try dragging it from the middle with the mouse to move it.

Or drag one of the handles to resize it.

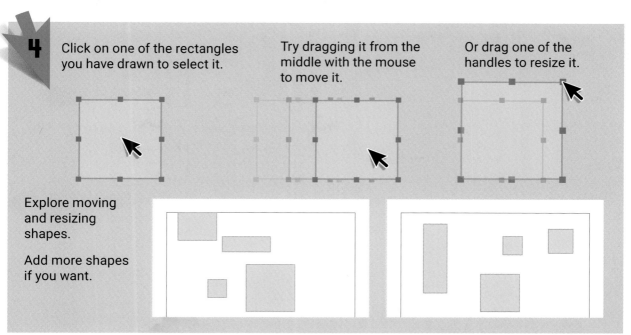

Explore moving and resizing shapes.

Add more shapes if you want.

5 To change the colour of a shape, click it to select it.

Find the drop-down menu next to **Colour** in the toolbar, then choose a colour.

Try changing the colours of all the shapes on your page.

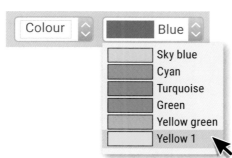

Colour ⬍ | Blue ⬍

Sky blue
Cyan
Turquoise
Green
Yellow green
Yellow 1

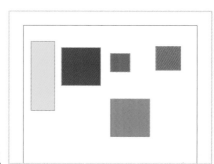

Explore and experiment

Experiment with the techniques you have learnt so far. You could also try arranging, rotating, copying and pasting your shapes. Turn to page 21 for help.

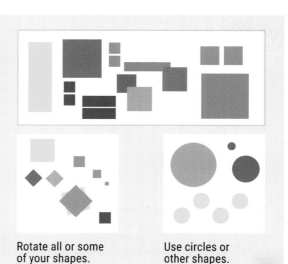

Try layering your shapes on top of each other in a pattern.

Copy and paste groups of shapes by holding down **'Shift'** when selecting.

Rotate all or some of your shapes.

Use circles or other shapes.

DICE NET

You can use vector graphics for more than just making pictures: you can also use them to draw nets, or patterns, that you can print out and make into objects. In this activity, we will make a cube net that folds into a dice.

1 Start up your vector graphics program.

File
- Text Document
- Spreadsheet
- Presentation
- **Drawing**
- Database
- Formula

2 On the **Drawing** toolbar, click the **Rectangle** tool.

Drag out a square shape to make one face of the dice.

Hold down the **'Shift'** key while you draw to make sure you create an exact square, not a rectangle.

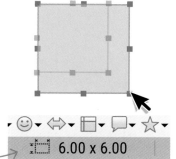

3 The square needs to be the right size, so we can fit 5 more on the page.

Hold down the **'Shift'** key again.

Carefully drag a corner green handle until the square is exactly **6 x 6 cm**.

The size of the square will be shown at the bottom of the page in the centre.

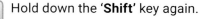

6.00 x 6.00

4 Now we will change the colour of the square. Hover the mouse over the drop-down menu to the right of **Colour**. While you hover, this will show up:

Area Style/Filling

Choose your dice colour.

Colour — Blue
- Yellow
- Orange
- **Red**
- Pink
- Magenta
- Purple

5 Make sure the square is still selected. If necessary, click it so it has green handles.

Now duplicate the square:

Click the **Edit** menu then **Copy**.

Click the **Edit** menu then **Paste**.

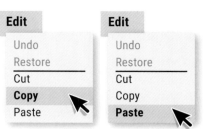

6 Drag the new square down so it just touches the bottom edge of the first square.

Use the **cursor keys** on your keyboard to nudge the square into place. Make sure it is lined up precisely.

7 Copy and paste to create 6 squares, then arrange as shown.

Click **Undo** if you make a mistake.

If you want to add tabs to your dice net, use the **Trapezoid** tool.

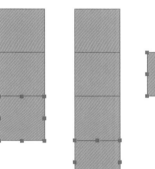

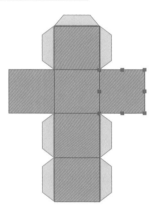

8 On the **Drawing** toolbar, click the **Ellipse** tool.

Drag out a circle to make the dot.

Hold down '**Shift**' to make it round.

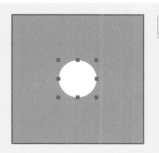
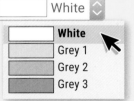

Colour the dot white. Use **Copy** and **Paste** to duplicate the spot and complete the dice net as shown.

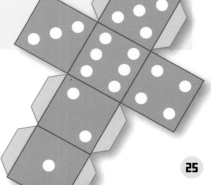

Print out your net.

Cut it out and fold it up. Glue together using the tabs. Roll the dice!

25

BIRTHDAY CARD

Do you know anyone with a birthday coming up? Let's draw them a unique birthday card. To make sure everything is in the right place, we will be drawing layout lines, and learning how to turn text upside down.

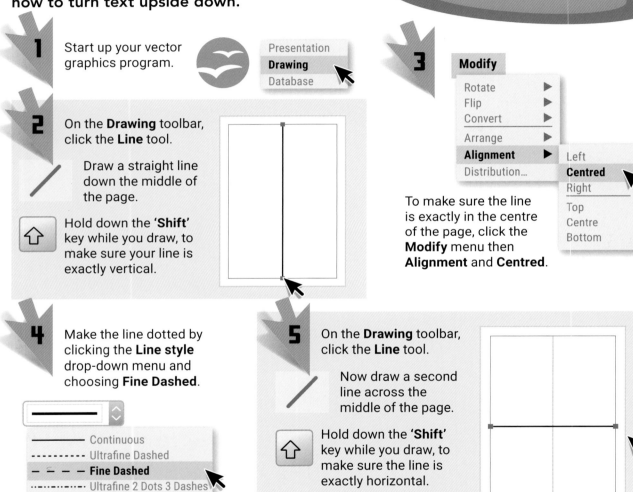

1 Start up your vector graphics program.

Presentation
Drawing
Database

2 On the **Drawing** toolbar, click the **Line** tool.

Draw a straight line down the middle of the page.

Hold down the **'Shift'** key while you draw, to make sure your line is exactly vertical.

3

Modify

Rotate ▶
Flip ▶
Convert ▶
Arrange ▶
Alignment ▶
Distribution…

Left
Centred
Right
Top
Centre
Bottom

To make sure the line is exactly in the centre of the page, click the **Modify** menu then **Alignment** and **Centred**.

4 Make the line dotted by clicking the **Line style** drop-down menu and choosing **Fine Dashed**.

——————— Continuous
- - - - - - - Ultrafine Dashed
– – – – Fine Dashed
—·—·—·— Ultrafine 2 Dots 3 Dashes
············· Fine Dotted

5 On the **Drawing** toolbar, click the **Line** tool.

Now draw a second line across the middle of the page.

Hold down the **'Shift'** key while you draw, to make sure the line is exactly horizontal.

6 To make sure it is exactly in the centre, click the **Modify** menu, then **Alignment** and **Centre**.

Left
Centred
Right
Top
Centre
Bottom

7 Make the line dotted by repeating step 4.

When you print out your card, fold on the dotted lines. This means the inside message section will need to be written upside down. The front is the bottom right quarter.

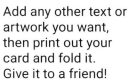
әpis**u**ı
Front

8

Now we will draw a cake in the front quarter. See step 4 on page 24 for help with choosing colours.

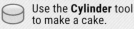

Use the **Ellipse** tool to draw a green plate.

Use the **Cylinder** tool to make a cake.

Zoom in and use the **Rectangle** tool to make a candle.

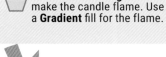

Colour	
None	
Colour	
Gradient	
Hatching	

Draw a thin **Pentagon** to make the candle flame. Use a **Gradient** fill for the flame.

Hold down **'Shift'** then click both the candle and the flame. Click **Edit**, then **Copy**.

Click **Edit**, then **Paste** to add candles. Drag them into place.

TIP: If you want to insert a picture you have already drawn, click **Insert, Picture** then **From File**.

Or **Copy** one of your own photos, then click **Paste**.

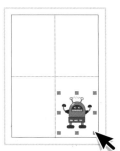

Use the handles to resize the picture. It should fit in the bottom right quarter.

Hold the **'Shift'** key to keep the proportions of the picture.

9

On the **Drawing** toolbar, click the **Text** tool.

Click the place where you want to add text.

Type in your text.　　Happy Birthday!|

Highlight the text.　　Happy Birthday!

Choose a font.　　American Typewriter ▼

Set the size.　　28 ▼

Set the colour.　　A▼

Happy Birthday!

10

Click the **Text** tool again.

Click here and type your message.

Click the blue edge of the text box until red handles appear.

■ Happy Birthday
■ Love from
■ Linus

Drag a red handle to spin the text round...

Happy Birthday
Love from
Linus

...until it is upside down!

Linus
Love from
Happy Birthday

11

Add any other text or artwork you want, then print out your card and fold it. Give it to a friend!

Happy Birthday!

POSE FOR A PORTRAIT

Now we are going to create a vector portrait. We will start with a photo, but simplify it considerably by removing the detail and choosing just a few lines, shapes and colours. By doing this activity, you will learn how to use layers and how to make more complex shapes.

1 Start by looking at vector portraits created by other artists. Ask an adult if you can use the Internet, then search for **'vector portraits'**. Click **'Images'**. Here are some examples of what you might find:

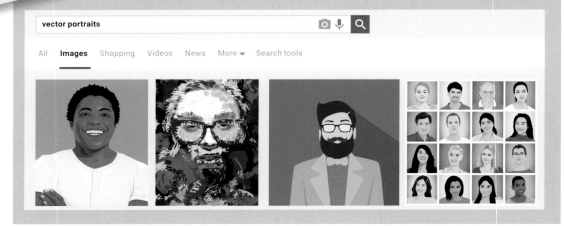

2 Take a photo of yourself, or a friend if they are going to be the subject of your vector portrait. You need to import the photo to your computer, or you could use a web-cam if your computer has one. Turn to page 35 for help.

3 Start up your vector graphics program.

Presentation
Drawing
Database

4 Click the **Insert** menu then **Picture** and **From File**.

Browse for your photo. Then click **Open** or **OK**.

Insert

Formatting Mark ▶
Hyperlink
Picture ▶ From File...
Table...   Scan
Movie and Sound
Object ▶

If you can't find your photo, import it again, or look in your **Documents**, **Pictures** or **Recent documents** folders.

Your photo should now appear on the page.

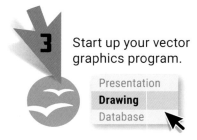

5 To stop the photo from moving around when we are working on it, we will lock it in place:

Double-click the **Layout** tab at the bottom of the screen, in the middle.

We can now edit the properties of the layer.

Tick the **Locked** option, then click **OK**.

Now the Layout layer with the photo on it will be locked in place.

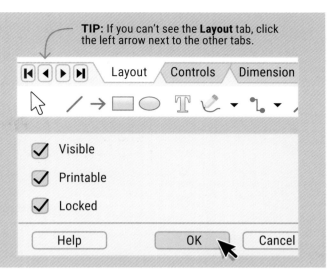

6 Click the **Insert** menu then **Layer** to make another layer for the portrait.

Insert
- Slide
- Duplicate Slide
- **Layer...**
- Insert Snap Point/Line...
- Fields ▶

Type in **'portrait'** then click **OK**.

Name
portrait
Title

Description

7 Now we can start drawing our vector portait over the top of the photo, but on our new layer called 'portrait'.

We still need to see the photo so we will make our drawing transparent.

Click the **Area** button.

Click the **Transparency** option.
Click **OK**.

Click the **Transparency** tab.

Area | Shadow | Transparency | Colours

Transparency Mode
- ○ No transparency
- ● Transparency   50% ⬍
- ○ Gradient

8 We need to choose a special **Curve** drawing tool to draw the features with:

Layout | Controls | Dimension

Click the **'Free-form line, filled'** tool.

Click here to choose from the different curve drawing options:

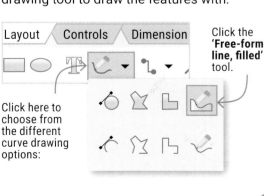

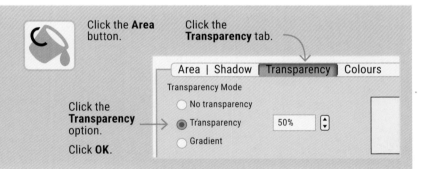

9 Use the zoom control in the bottom right of the window to zoom in. This will make it easier for you to draw the eyes.

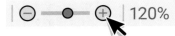

10 Click the special **Curve** tool.

Start drawing carefully around the outline of one eye.

Click **Undo** if you go wrong, then try again.

 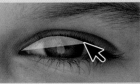   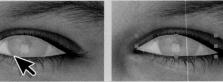

Release the mouse button when you get back to the start.

11 Draw the other eye, ears, nostrils and lips.

Your portrait may look better if you draw two lips, not one whole mouth, and nostrils, not the nose.

But don't worry if your portrait looks strange at this point. You may look a little like an alien!

You may have to select the **Curve** tool each time.

12 If you need to adjust any of the features, click the **Points** button on the toolbar at the bottom.

Use the mouse to carefully move the individual points that make up the curve. Use **Undo** if you make a mistake.

13 Scroll and zoom the page so you can see the hair. Carefully and slowly, draw round it.

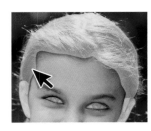

14 Zoom out again so you can see the whole head. Carefully draw round it. Imagine where the skull is: it will overlap the hair.

15 Now we will hide the photo. Double-click the **Layout** tab.

TIP: If you can't see the **Layout** tab, click the left arrow next to the other tabs.

Make the whole Layout layer invisible by turning **off** the **Visible** tick.

Click **OK**.

☐ Visible
☑ Printable
☑ Locked

Help   OK

---

16 Your art should now look like this:

Because we drew the head last, it will be on top of the other features. To change this we will send it to the back of the pile of things we have drawn.

Click the chin. Make sure you select the head, not the hair. **Right-click** it (on a Mac, hold '**Ctrl**' and **click**), then choose **Arrange** and **Send to Back**.

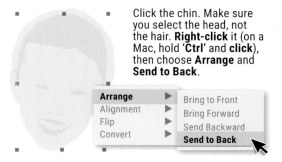

Arrange   ▶   Bring to Front
Alignment   ▶   Bring Forward
Flip   ▶   Send Backward
Convert   ▶   **Send to Back**

---

17 Now you can start colouring your portrait:

Click the **Area** button.

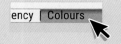

Choose the **Colours** tab.

Set the colour.

Choose the **Transparency** tab.

Transparency Mode
◉ No transparency
○ Transparency
○ Gradient

Choose **No transparency**.

---

18 Colour each part of the portrait to complete it.

Explore and experiment

Draw eyebrows and a neck.

Draw thick black lines around shapes.

Try a simple background.

Make new shapes with darker and lighter colours to give depth.

Try other colours.

PHOTO CUBE

This photo cube would make a great present for a parent or grandparent! To make it, we'll combine what we have learnt about making a cube with some work on photos. The photos could be of you and your family, your friends, animals, cars or anything you like.

1 Start up your vector graphics program.

Presentation
Drawing
Database

2 Find six photos that you want to use. Make copies of the photos in one folder by opening them and clicking **'Save as'**.

If you are using photos from the Internet, check with an adult, then download the photos into one folder.

Cube photos

12530371.jpg
101525437.jpg
104301419.jpg
128729591.jpg
137844992.jpg
144901279.jpg

3 On a **PC**, right-click the first photo. Click **Open with** then **Paint**.

Open with   **Paint**

Click **Select**.
Drag out a square selection box.

You need to check the dimensions to make sure the selection is square.

890 x 890

Click **Copy**.

On a **Mac**, double-click the first photo. It will open in **Preview**.

Drag out a square selection box.

Hold down the **'Shift'** key to make sure it is exactly square.

Edit

Cut
Copy

Click the **Edit** menu then **Copy**.

4 In your vector graphics program, click **Edit** and **Paste**. The photo should now be on your page.

Edit

Cut
Copy
Paste

5 We need to shrink the photo. It has to be done very accurately so that when we fold up the cube it will fit together properly. Instead of adjusting the size by using the green handles, find the dimensions at the bottom of the screen in the middle.

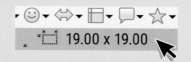

19.00 x 19.00

Double-click the dimensions.

TIP: If you can't see the dimensions or any numbers at the bottom of the screen, click **View** and check there is a tick next to the **Status bar**.

6 Type in the dimensions. Set **Width** to **6** and **Height** to **6**. (You don't need to type 'cm'.)

Position and Size	Rotation

Position
Position X   0.44 cm
Position Y   12.44 cm
Size
Width   6
Height   6

Click **OK**.

The picture will now be the right size to fit 5 more on the page.

7 Now repeat steps 3 to 6 for each of the other 5 photos.

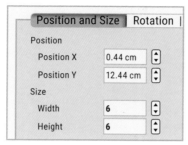

Use the **cursor keys** to nudge each photo into place. Make sure they are all lined up precisely as shown below.

8 Our photo cube is now almost complete. If you want to add some text to one or more of the sides of the cube, double-click that side and type a message.

See page 25 for help if you want to add tabs to your cube net before you print it out.

Cut out your net and fold it. Glue your photo cube together using the tabs.

Explore and experiment

Why not add speech bubbles to the photos?

Click the **Callouts** tool and choose your bubble.

Drag the yellow handle to move the 'tail' of the speech bubble to the mouth.

Click inside the speech bubble to type your message.

Hello Grandpa!

3 PHOTO FUN

In this chapter, we will find out how to do some creative photo-editing. We will be making artwork using photos and learning how to create special effects by combining digital images. First of all, let's take a look at the basics.

How photos are stored

Photos are stored as bitmaps on computers, so each part of a photograph is a pixel, just like in our first chapter.

However, one of the main differences from bitmap painting is the number of colours involved. When you are painting a bitmap picture you might use 10 or 20 different colours. In a photograph, there may be millions of slightly different colours.

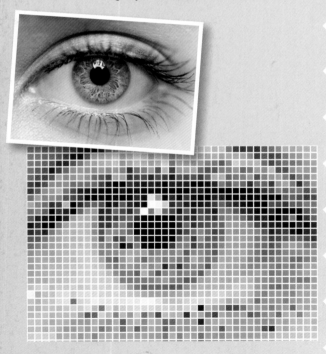

What software can I use?

Most cameras and smart phones enable you to do simple photo-editing and create special effects. Many websites let you do basic editing. But these don't really teach you how photo-editing works, or give you much flexibility. They are a bit like heating up a ready meal – but we will be teaching you how to cook!

For these projects, we will be using **Microsoft Paint** to do our photo-editing. This is a free program that you will already have on your computer if it is a PC or laptop that runs Windows. Turn to pages 76-77 for more information.

For Mac users and more advanced photo-editing

If you are using a Mac, unfortunately there is no free photo-editing software exactly equivalent to Microsoft Paint. With an adult's help, you could try downloading **Paint X Lite**, which is free. See pages 76–7 for more information. With Paint X Lite, you will be able to carry out all the photo-editing activities in this chapter, apart from 'Pop Art poster' on pages 46–9, and 'Digital graffiti' on pages 50–51. This is because Paint X Lite does not allow you to save as 16- or 2-colour bitmaps. Another difference is that you will need to zoom using the **View** menu or tab.

To carry out all the activities in this chapter, you may want to discuss with an adult the possibility of buying a more advanced program, such as **Photoshop**. See page 77 for advice on trying before you buy. For PC-users who want to go further, Photoshop will also make certain things simpler to do.

If you do your projects in Photoshop, turn to page 79 to find out how to use some of its different tools and options. Other programs, such as **PaintShop Pro**, **Photoshop Elements**, **Pixlr** and **Paint.net**, work in a similar way to Photoshop.

Getting photos onto your computer

First of all, make sure you know how to load photos onto your computer. Turn to page 78 for extra help.

Depending on your phone, camera and computer, the way you get photos on to the computer will be different. If you are using a phone, you may be able to transfer a photo by emailing it to yourself. There may be a program on your computer that 'syncs' with your phone.

If you are using a digital camera, there may be a cable, or an SD card, that you can plug into your computer. Some cameras use WiFi or Bluetooth to transfer images.

Photo use and safety

Always ask an adult before searching on the Internet for images. The work of most photographers and artists is protected by copyright. If you are looking for free-to-use images, search on sites such as **https://commons.wikimedia.org** or **https:// pixabay.com/**. For these activities, you need to use fairly high-resolution images, of at least 400 KB (400 kilobytes). Ask permission before you use photos of friends or family. Never upload photos of yourself or friends to the Internet, but do display these fantastic projects in the classroom or at home!

Resizing photos

Digital photos come in different sizes. High-resolution photographs have more pixels and therefore more detail. They take up more memory on a computer, and take longer to email. However, they will print out at much better quality.

Many cameras take photographs with many millions of pixels. A camera that takes 10 MB (10 megabyte) photos will create pictures that are around 4000 x 2500 pixels. Most computer screens have only around a quarter of those pixels. Although you can edit big photos, it may be slow. For the projects in this chapter, you will find it useful to resize large photos.

Resizing in Microsoft Paint

Click **Resize**.

Choose **Pixels**.

Type **400** (or the size you want the picture) in the **Vertical** box. When it is resized, your photo will keep the same proportions.

Then click **OK**.

Resize		
Percentage	⦿	Pixels
Horizontal:		188
Vertical:		**400**

FLYING LESSONS

Learning to fly is much easier with a bit of computer trickery. In this activity, we will learn how to turn a photo of someone sitting on a broomstick into a soaring work of art. To do this, we will carefully remove the background of the photo, and then paste it onto a photo of a stormy sky. Hold on tight!

1 Ask a friend to take a photo of you riding a broomstick! Make sure they take it from the side.

You will need to get the photo onto your computer (see page 35 for help).

2 We are going to use **Microsoft Paint** but you could use other software.

Find your photo file on the computer.

Image 159.jpg

Then **right-click** the photo.

Click **Open with** then **Paint**.

Open with **Paint**

3 You will probably need to resize the photo to make it easier to work with.

 Resize

Click **Resize**.

Choose **Pixels**.

Resize	
Percentage	⦿ Pixels
Horizontal:	370
Vertical:	400

Type **400**. Click **OK**.

The picture should fit on the screen.

4 Click the **File** menu then **Save**.

File
New
Open
Save

Call the picture **broomstick**.

File name: **broomstick**

Click **Save**.

Save

TIP: Don't just save your work when it is finished. Save it early on during an activity, then keep saving every few minutes. By doing that, all the changes you make will be saved too.

5 We will start by roughly 'chopping off' big parts of the background.

Click **Select**.

Select part of the background and press the **'Delete'** key.

Repeat with more rectangles until you have roughly removed most of the background.

TIP: Click **Undo** if you make a mistake. Then try again!

6 Zoom in with the **Slider** at the bottom right of the screen, or use the **Magnifier** on the **View** tab.

7 Click **Select**.

Choose **Free-form selection**.

Select ▼   ◯ Free-form selection

Make a selection and press **'Delete'**.

Carefully select and delete the other parts of the background until only the broomstick and rider are left.

Only select small parts each time – that way, if you accidentally delete part of the rider, you can use **Undo**!

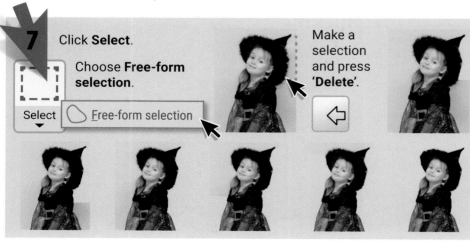

8 Now you could use one of your own photos of the sky, preferably on a stormy evening. If that's not possible, ask an adult if you can use the Internet.

You need to find a photograph of a stormy sky that is in the public domain. See page 35 for help finding one.

Right-click the image then click **Copy**.

Save
Copy

Then close the web browser.

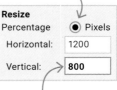

9 Start another copy of Microsoft Paint by clicking the Windows **Start** button and then clicking **Paint**.

10 Click **Paste** to add the photo.

TIP: **If the photo is too small:** Go back to step 8 and choose another photo.
Make sure you don't copy the photo from the results page with all the pictures on. Click the photo you want – this will usually take you to a larger copy. Now copy this larger version.

TIP: **If the photo is too big:** The photo needs to be around 800 pixels high to fit on a typical computer screen. If you can only see part of the photo, you need to resize it.

 Resize

Click **Resize**.

Choose **Pixels**.

Resize	
Percentage	⦿ Pixels
Horizontal:	1200
Vertical:	**800**

Type **800**. Then click **OK**.

The exact height you need depends on your screen. Experiment to see what looks best.

11 Switch back to the first copy of Microsoft Paint by holding down the **'Alt'** key (next to the space bar) and tapping the **'Tab'** key.

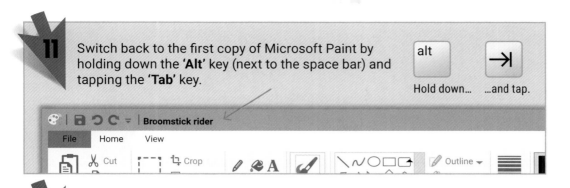

alt

Hold down...

→|

...and tap.

12 We need to copy the broomstick rider so we can add it to the cloudy sky.

Click **Select**, then choose **Select all**.

Click **Copy**.

Click **Save** before you close the file just in case you need it again.

Click **Close**.

13 You should now see the stormy sky in Microsoft Paint. Use **'Alt'** and **'Tab'** if you don't.

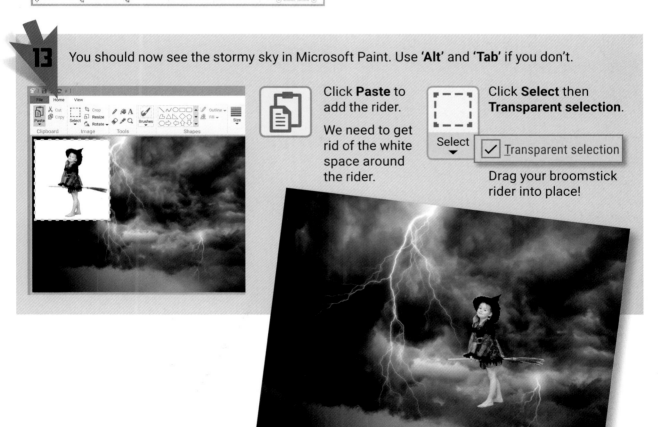

Click **Paste** to add the rider.

We need to get rid of the white space around the rider.

Click **Select** then **Transparent selection**.

Drag your broomstick rider into place!

BECOME AN ASTRONAUT

In this activity, we will edit and blend two photographs to make it look as if you are an astronaut. To do this, we will remove the visor from a helmet in a photograph of an astronaut, then make it transparent. By copying and pasting this photo over the top of a photo of yourself, you will be ready to travel into space!

1 Start by asking an adult if you can use the Internet. Search for a photograph of an astronaut that is in the public domain (see page 35 for help).

This is NASA astronaut Buzz Aldrin on the Moon, photographed by Neil Armstrong on 20 July 1969.

Right-click the image then click **Copy**.

Save
Copy

2 Start up your painting program. We are going to use **Microsoft Paint**, but you could use other software.

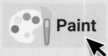
🎨 Paint

3 Click **Paste** to add the image.

4 Zoom in with the **Slider**, or the **Magnifier** on the **View** tab.

Move the scroll bars so the helmet is filling the screen.

200%

5 We need to rub out the whole of the visor in the helmet.

 Click the **Select** tool.

Carefully drag out a dotted selection rectangle in the middle of the helmet.

6 Press the **'Delete'** key.

The middle of the helmet should now be white.

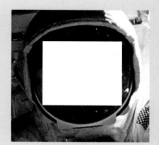

7 Now we need to rub out the rest of the visor. We could use the Rubber, but it is square and jagged. The round brush will give a smoother finish.

Click the **Brushes** tool.

Choose the thickest brush.

Choose white as the main colour.

8 Slowly paint round the edge of the helmet until it is all white.

Paint a small section, then let go of the mouse. Then paint some more. That way, if you make a mistake you can use **Undo** to take back the last brush stroke only.

9 We need to resize the picture so most of it fits on the screen. The bigger it is, the better the quality will be, but it may be harder to work on.

Resize
Click **Resize**.

Choose **Pixels**.

Resize		
Percentage	○	● Pixels
Horizontal:	871	
Vertical:	**1000**	

Type **1000**. Click **OK**.

Most of the picture should fit on the screen.

10 We need to make two copies of the astronaut picture, one for the back of our final image, and one for the front. We will sandwich your own photo inbetween.

File
New
Open
Save

Click the **File** menu then **Save**.

File name: **astronaut top**

Call the picture **'astronaut top'**.

Save
Click **Save**.

11 Click the **File** menu then **Save as**.

File
New
Open
Save
Save as

Call this picture **'astronaut back'**.

File name: **astronaut back**

Click **Save**.
Save

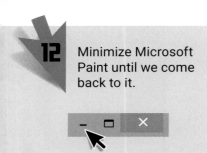

12 Minimize Microsoft Paint until we come back to it.

13 Find a photo to use in the helmet. Choose one where you are looking forwards so it matches the astronaut's pose.

Right-click the photo. Click **Open with** then **Paint**.

Open with ••• **Paint**

14 Click **Select**.

Click **Select all**.

Select ▼ ☐ Select all

Click **Copy**.

Close the photo file.

15 Switch back to the **astronaut back** copy of Microsoft Paint by holding down the '**Alt**' key (next to the space bar) and tapping the '**Tab**' key.

alt →|

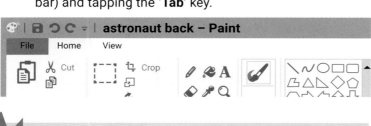

🎨 | 🖫 ⟳ ⟲ ⩲ | **astronaut back – Paint**

File   Home   View

16 Click **Paste** to add your own photo.

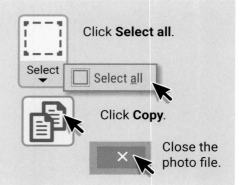

17 We need to shrink down the new photo so it roughly fits the helmet.

 Resize

Click **Resize**.

Choose **Percentage**.

Resize
● Percentage ○ Pixels
Horizontal: 50
Vertical: **50**

Type **50**.

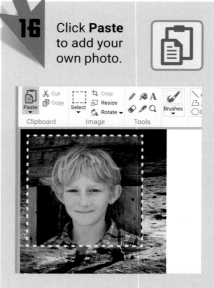

18

To make the face match more precisely, use the handles in the corner of the photo to resize it.

Then move it carefully so it is over the hole in the helmet.

19

We need to get the **astronaut top** file back.

Start another copy of Microsoft Paint by clicking the Windows **Start** button and then clicking **Paint**.

 Paint

File	
New	**Recent pictures**
Open	**1 astronaut top**
Save	2 astronaut back

Open the **astronaut top** file.

20

Click **Select** then **Select all**.

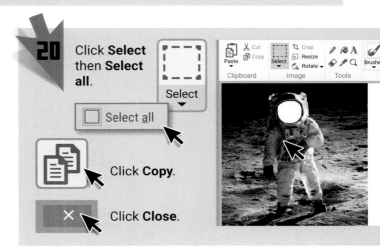

Click **Copy**.

Click **Close**.

22

Finally, drag your spacesuit into place.

21

You should now be back in the **astronaut back** file.

Click **Paste**.

Click **Select** then **Transparent selection**.

Select
✓ Transparent selection

DINOSAUR DISASTER

Now we will use some of the techniques we have learnt to create a picture of a friend being chased by... a dinosaur! You'll need to find an artwork of a dinosaur, then get a friend to strike a photo pose that looks as if they are running from something terrifying. We'll combine the two images to create a fearsome result!

1 Ask an adult to help you find an image of a dinosaur that is in the public domain (see page 35 for help).

Right-click the image then click **Copy**.

2 Start **Microsoft Paint**.

Paste the dinosaur image.

It should fill most of the screen. If it is the wrong size, see page 38 for help.

3 Click the **File** menu then **Save**.

Call the picture **'dinosaur'**.

File name: dinosaur

Click **Save**.

4 Ask a friend to take a photo of you, or the other way round. Pose as if you are running for your life!

You will need to get the photo on to your computer (see page 35 for help).

5 Find your photo file on the computer.

Right-click the photo. Click **Open with** then **Paint**.

Open with

Image 162.jpg

6 You will probably need to resize the photo to make it smaller.

Click **Resize**.

Resize
Percentage ○ ● Pixels
Horizontal: 300
Vertical: 400

Choose **Pixels**.

Type **400**. Then click **OK**.

7 Use the **Select** tool to remove the background of this photo (follow the instructions on page 37 for a reminder).

Select ▼

Use the **Undo** button if you delete too much. **Save** your photo.

Free-form selection

8 Now we need to copy the running person to add them to the dinosaur image.

Click **Select**, then choose **Select all**.

Select ▼ ☐ Select a**l**l

Click **Copy**. Finally, you should click **Close**.

Copy

✕

9 Click **Paste** to add the running person to your dinosaur image.

To get rid of the white space around the person, click **Select**.

Choose **Transparent selection**.

Select ▼ ✓ Transparent selection

Drag the person in front of the dinosaur!

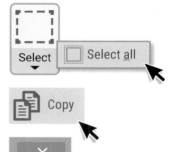

POP ART POSTER

Many artists have used the idea of repeating the same image in their work, playing around with different colours. From the 1950s, Andy Warhol and other artists in the Pop Art movement explored how they could use screen printing to get the effect. Today's artists, such as Russell Marshall, use digital technology. In this activity, you will create our own digital artwork using repetition.

1 Start by looking at some examples of Pop Art or the work of Russell Marshall. Ask an adult if you can use the Internet. Click '**Images**'.

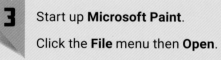

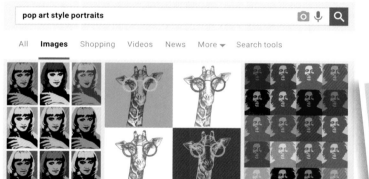

2 Take a photo of yourself, or a friend if they are going to be the subject of your Pop Art poster. The photo needs to have a strong contrast between you and the background.

Why not take a portrait of yourself against a wall that is a paler colour than your hair and skin.

You need to import the photo to your computer, or you could use a web-cam.

3 Start up **Microsoft Paint**.

Click the **File** menu then **Open**.

Browse for your photo, then click **OK**.

4 Next we need to resize the photo as it will be much too large to work with easily.

Click **Resize**.

Choose **Pixels**.

Resize	
Percentage	● Pixels
Horizontal:	376
Vertical:	500

Type **500**. Then click **OK**. Now the photo should be about half the screen height.

5

We will need to change parts of the picture one dot – one pixel – at a time.

Choose the **Fill** tool and try colouring parts of the image. You will only be able to change a tiny part of it. This is because Fill looks for pixels that are the same colour, and there may be millions of different colours in a photo.

Normal   *16-colour*   *Monochrome*

To make artwork we can re-colour, we need to change the picture to be in 16 colours or monochrome (2 colours – black and white).

6

Click the **File** menu then **Save as**.

File

New
Open
Save
Save as

File name: **stamp**

Save as type: JPEG (*.jpg;*.jpeg)
Monochrome Bitmap
16 Colour Bitmap

Type in a file name.

Choose the file type **Monochrome bitmap**.

Click **Save**.

 Save

7

Your screen should now look like this:

Click **Select**, then choose **Select all**.

Select
☐ Select all

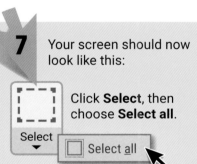

Click **Copy**.

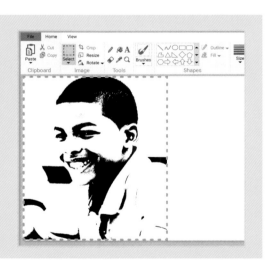

8

Start a new file for your artwork.

Click the **File** menu then **Properties**.

File

New
Open

Properties

Set the size of the new file to be around **1200** x **500** pixels.

Width: **1200**   Height: **500**

Click **OK**.

9 Click **Paste** to add the monochrome photo.

Move the photo to where you want it to be placed in your picture.

10 Choose the **Fill** tool and pick a colour.

Colour the image by clicking on it.

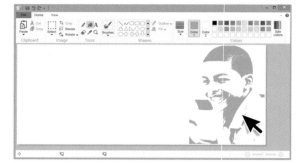

11 Click **Paste** to add another image.

Move the photo to where you want it to be placed in your picture.

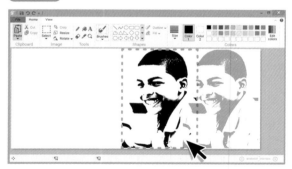

12 The white background of the new image may rub out parts of the first photo.

To prevent that happening:

Click **Select**.

Click **Transparent selection**.

Select ▼

✓ Transparent selection

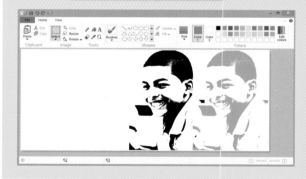

13 Repeat steps 10, 11 and 12 to add more images and colour them.

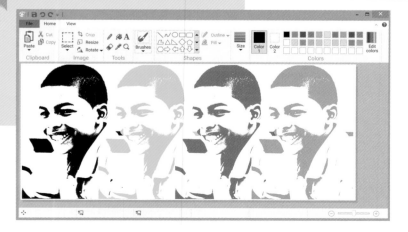

Your artwork is now complete! **Save** and **print** it out.

Explore and experiment

Instead of repeating the same image, you could use a group of similar images. How about photos of your friends, animals or racing cars?

Start a new file and draw some coloured squares. Save it as **'squares'**.

Repeat steps 3–7 for each photo, then paste them into the 'squares' file.

By saving the original photo as 16-colour instead of monochrome, you get a very different effect.

Start a new file and draw some coloured rectangles. Save it as **'rectangles'**.

Follow steps 3–7, but at step 6 save as **'16-colour bitmap'**. Paste the images into the 'rectangles' file.

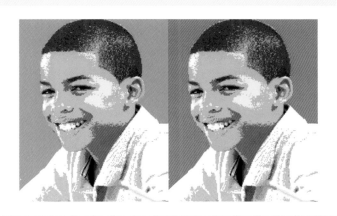

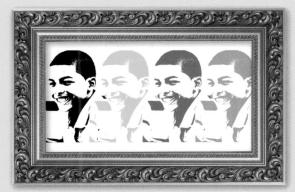

You could print out your picture and put it in an old picture frame.

If you don't have a real picture frame, try searching for a photo of one. You could copy and paste the photo into Microsoft Paint, then go back to your artwork. Select it, copy it and paste it on top of the photo frame. You'll need to use the handles to resize it.

Alternatively, why not make a group of small pictures and put them in photo frames (or photos of photo frames).

Artists call a group of three pictures a triptych.

DIGITAL GRAFFITI

Some artists use stencils and spray paint to create pieces of street art or graffiti. A French artist named Blek le Rat was one of the pioneers of this technique. In the UK, artists like Banksy use stencils to repeat parts of an artwork. We'll be looking at how we can use these ideas to create a piece of digital graffiti – without getting in trouble for spraying anyone's wall.

1 Start by looking at some examples of stencilled street art. Ask an adult if you can use the Internet, then search for '**Banksy**' or '**Blek le Rat**'. Click '**Images**'. Here are some examples of images you might find:

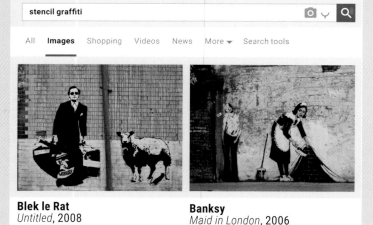

Blek le Rat
Untitled, 2008

Banksy
Maid in London, 2006

2 First you need a photo of a brick wall. Either take a photo or ask an adult to help you look for a public domain photo on the Internet (see page 35 for help). Load it onto your computer.

3 Start up **Microsoft Paint**.

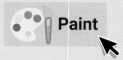

4 Click the **File** menu, then **Open**. Browse for your photo, then click **OK**.

5 Next we need to resize the photo to make it fit on the screen.

Click **Resize**.

Choose **Pixels**.

Resize		
Percentage	○	● Pixels
Horizontal:		1100
Vertical:		700

Type **700**. Then click **OK**. Now the picture should all fit on the screen.

6

Now we need to find an image to stencil onto the wall. Either take a photo or look for an image on the Internet. Ask an adult for help.

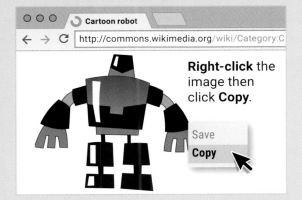

Right-click the image then click **Copy**.

Save

Copy

7

Start up another copy of Microsoft Paint.

Click **Paste** to add the image.

If the image doesn't fit on the screen, resize it so it is about the same size as the wall (see step 5 for help).

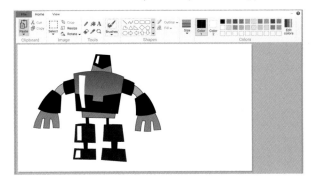

8

We need to reduce the number of colours in our stencil art.

Click the **File** menu then **Save**.

File

New

Open

Save

Type in a file name.

Choose the file type **Monochrome bitmap**.

Click **Save**.

File name:	**robot**
Save as type:	JPEG (*.jpg;*.jpeg)
	Monochrome Bitmap
	16 Colour Bitmap

9

The image will now be black and white.

Click the **Select** tool.

Draw a dotted selection box around the image.

Click **Copy**.

10

Switch back to your other copy of Microsoft Paint by holding down the '**Alt**' key (next to the space bar) and tapping the '**Tab**' key.

alt   →|

Click **Paste**.

Choose where to put your stencil on the wall and resize it if you need to.

11

Repeat step 10 to add more copies of the image. Repeat steps 6 to 10 to add other images. Choose **Fill** then click on an image to change its colour.

4 MAKING ANIMATIONS

We are used to seeing animations in films, TV shows and computer games. Whether created on a computer, drawn by hand or made with clay models, all animation works on the same principle. A series of images are shown in quick succession, with slight changes between each image. This tricks our brains into thinking something is really moving.

What software can I use?

You can try creating stop-frame animation with a camera and some software (with an adult's help, search online for **'stop frame animation software'** or **'stop frame animation apps'**). In this chapter, we are going to draw our own animation frames in **Scratch**, which is free software that you can use on PCs, Macs and Linux computers. For help with accessing the Scratch website, or downloading Scratch to your computer, turn to page 77.

How animations work

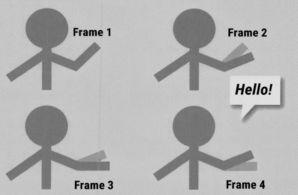

Frame 1
Frame 2
Hello!
Frame 3
Frame 4

Using Scratch

Click **Try it out**, then familiarize yourself with how the Scratch screen looks:

TRY IT OUT

Showing these four pictures, or frames, quickly one after the other will make it look as though our stick person is waving. One of the important principles in animation is to make small changes between each picture. If we used only two frames in this arm-waving animation it would look jerky. If we used eight frames, we could make the arm move only a degree or two between each frame, and the result would be much smoother.

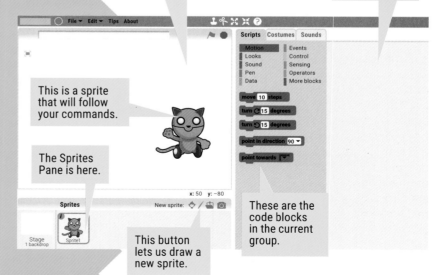

This is the Stage, where you watch your animations.

This is the Scripts Area, where you drag your code.

This is a sprite that will follow your commands.

The Sprites Pane is here.

This button lets us draw a new sprite.

These are the code blocks in the current group.

Creating animation frames

We will start by drawing the first frame. We will then duplicate, or copy, frame 1, to use it as a base to draw frame 2. We will keep on duplicating our last frame, then drawing the next one.

If you are animating the whole background, Scratch calls each frame a new **backdrop**. To duplicate a backdrop frame in Scratch:

 After you have drawn your first backdrop frame, in the centre of the screen, **right-click** the **backdrop1** icon. On a Mac, hold **'Ctrl'** then click.

Click **Duplicate**.

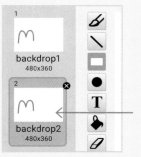 A new backdrop will appear below the first.

Now draw your second backdrop.

A character that moves around in front of the backdrop is called a sprite. If you are animating a sprite, Scratch calls each frame a new **costume**. To duplicate a costume frame in Scratch:

 After you have drawn your sprite, in the centre of the screen, **right-click** the **costume1** icon. On a Mac, hold **'Ctrl'** then click.

Click **Duplicate**.

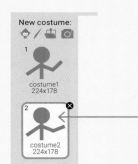 A new costume will appear below the first.

Now draw your second costume.

Changing frames

Our code needs to change frames quickly and automatically. To do this we will code a loop that runs some commands over and over again. The commands tell Scratch what to do. Commands in Scratch need to be dragged from different groups. The commands are all colour-coded to make this easier.

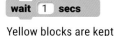

Brownish coloured blocks like this are kept in the **Events** group.

Purple blocks are found in the **Looks** group.

Yellow blocks are kept in the **Control** group.

Here is a simple program to make a sprite's costume frames change automatically:

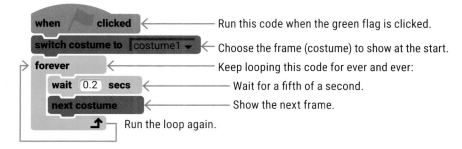

Run this code when the green flag is clicked.
Choose the frame (costume) to show at the start.
Keep looping this code for ever and ever:
Wait for a fifth of a second.
Show the next frame.
Run the loop again.

If we were animating the background we would use these purple commands instead:

53

ANIMATE YOUR NAME

As a simple introduction to animation we will do an activity that draws your name on the screen one letter at a time, and then makes it flash. Each letter is a separate frame in our animation. We will create each frame as a new backdrop in Scratch. We will use code to make each backdrop appear in turn.

1 Go to the Scratch website. Then click **Try it out**.

2 We don't need the standard Scratch cat sprite so we will delete it:

In the Sprites Pane, **right-click** the cat with the right mouse button. On a Mac, hold down the **'Ctrl'** key then click. Click **Delete**.

3 In the centre of the Scratch screen, click the **Backdrops** tab so we can draw a new background for the Stage area.

Scripts	Backdrops

New backdrop:

4 Use the mouse to slowly draw the first letter of your name.

Choose the **Brush** tool.

Use the slider to make the line nice and thick.

Select a colour.

Click the **Undo** button if you make a mistake!

5 We need to make the next letter. To avoid having to draw the first one again, we will duplicate it.

In the centre of the screen, **right-click** the **backdrop1** icon.

Click **Duplicate**.

A new backdrop will appear below the first.

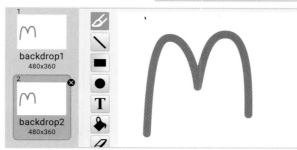

6 Now draw the second letter.

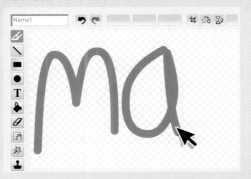

8 Keep repeating steps 6 and 7 until your name is finished.

7 Right-click **backdrop2** then click **Duplicate**.

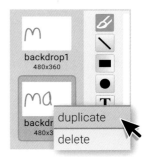

9 We can preview the animation by clicking the **backdrop1** and **backdrop2** icons to switch them.

However, to make the animation work properly we need to add code.

In the centre of the screen, click the **Scripts** tab. Click the **Control** group.

Drag a **'Forever'** code block over to the Scripts Area.

10 Drag a **'Wait 1 secs'** code block into the Forever loop.

 Click the **Events** group and drag a **'When green flag clicked'** block to the top of the code.

 Click the **Looks** group and drag a **'Switch backdrop to'** block under the **'When green flag clicked'** block. Set it to **backdrop1**.

Drag a **'Next backdrop'** block below **'Wait 1 secs'**.

Click the **Green flag** button at the top right of the Stage to test your animation!

when ▢ clicked
switch backdrop to backdrop1
forever
    wait 1 secs
    next backdrop

11 To make your name flash:

Duplicate the last backdrop.

Choose the **Fill** tool, and a colour.

Re-colour the letters.

Explore and experiment

Can you add more colours to your name?
Can you make it flash for longer?
Can you make the animation faster or slower?

12 Duplicate the red letter backdrop, and then the green one, until you have two or three of each.

 Click the **Green flag** again!

HAIR GROWER

Now we will create an animation of a cartoon character whose hair grows longer and longer. This time we will be animating a sprite rather than the background. We will create a series of costumes for our sprite, with increasingly long hair. We will use a coded loop to make each costume appear in turn.

1 Go to the Scratch website. Then click **Try it out**.

2 We will delete the standard Scratch cat sprite as we are drawing our own character.
In the Sprites Pane, **right-click** the cat with the right mouse button. On a Mac, hold down the **'Ctrl'** key then click. Click **Delete**.

3 Start your cartoon character by clicking the **'Paint new sprite'** button in the Sprites Pane.

4 We will draw a simple face, with no hair.

Choose the **Ellipse** tool.

Click the solid shape to make sure it is filled in.

 While you draw your face, hold the **'Shift'** key to make it a perfect circle.

Select a skin colour.

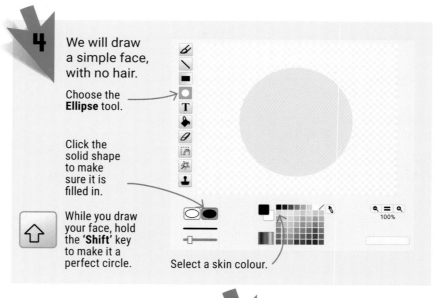

5 Add two small circles to be ears. Make two black circles for eyes.

6 Use the **Brush** to draw a mouth.

7 We need to make the next frame in the animation. Scratch calls this the next costume. To avoid drawing the face all over again, we will duplicate the first costume.

In the centre of the screen, **right-click** the **costume1** icon. Click **Duplicate**.

A new costume will appear below the first one.

8 Now draw the next costume.

Choose the **Brush** tool. Make the brush a bit thicker. Draw a little bit of hair.

9 **Right-click** and duplicate **costume2**.

10 For this costume, make the hair a little bit longer.

Then duplicate this costume by repeating step 9.

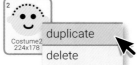

Keep repeating steps 9 and 10 until there are about 10 costumes.

11 We can preview the animation by clicking the costume1 and costume2 icons to switch between them. But to make the animation work properly, we need to add code:

In the centre of the screen, click the **Scripts** tab. Click the **Control** group.

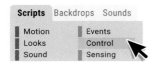

Drag a **'Forever'** code block over to the Scripts Area.

12 Drag a **'Wait 1 secs'** code block into the 'Forever' loop.

To make the animation work more quickly, change it to show **0.2** secs.

Click the **Events** group and drag a **'When green flag clicked'** block to the top of the code.

Click the **Looks** group and drag over a **'Switch costume to'** block. Set it to **costume1**.

Drag a **'Next costume'** block below the 'Wait' block.

Now click the **Green flag** button to test your animation!

GAME ANIMATION

We've seen how a sequence of pictures can be made into a short animation clip. Similar techniques can be combined with more code to create animated characters in a computer game. In this activity, we will draw a character, make it run across the screen, then add it to a simple game.

1 First of all, let's plan out our animation. We need to make four different pictures of a runner, which we will show one after the other every time the runner moves. The pictures will loop in a never-ending cycle. Professional animators call this a 'run cycle'.

In picture 1, the first foot is just in contact with the ground.

The first foot is now on the ground and the second leg is coming toward it. The arms have moved a bit and the body and head are lower.

The second leg is now coming past the first foot – you can see the knee sticking out. The arms are also further forward.

Now the second leg is pushing up and the head and body are higher up.

2 Start Scratch.

TRY IT OUT

In the Sprites Pane, **right-click** the cat. On a Mac, hold '**Ctrl**' and click. Click **Delete**.

3 Start to draw your character by clicking the '**Paint new sprite**' button.

New sprite:
Paint new sprite

4 We need to be able to move the character's arms and legs. Instead of using a bitmap to do this, we will draw the runner with vector graphics. In the bottom right of the screen click '**Convert to vector**'.

Bitmap Mode

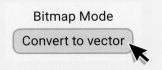

5 The drawing tools will be on the right of the screen.

Choose the **Ellipse** tool.

Draw a circle and make it **Solid**.

Draw a small circle at the top of the Drawing Area.

 TIP: Click **Undo** if you make a mistake. Then try again!

6 Choose the **Line** tool.

Make it thick.

Draw a line for the body.

Draw a leg.

Add a foot.

Start the other leg. Draw it up to the knee.

Draw another line joining the knee.

Add the foot.

7 Draw one arm, then the other.

8 Adjust your stick runner if it is not quite correct.

 Choose the **Reshape** tool. Click an arm and round handles will appear.

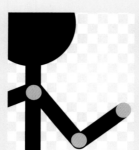

It needs to look like me!

Drag the handles carefully to reshape the arm or leg.

TIP: The **Reshape** tool lets you move the handles around by dragging them. If you click one of the handles you will delete it. Add new handles by clicking Reshape then clicking a line.

9 **Duplicate** this first frame (**costume1**) in the animation.

10 Adjust the runner in the second frame so it looks like this.

You need to use the **Reshape** tool to move the handles.

You will need to create a new handle on the knee by clicking on it. Then move the knee handle up and right.

Then move the foot down.

11 **Duplicate** the second frame (**costume2**) in the animation.

This will give you the third frame.

Use the **Reshape** tool to make the runner look like this.

12 The last frame will be quite like the first one.

 Duplicate costume1 and use the **Reshape** tool to make your runner look like this.

13 Click the **Scripts** tab. Add this code to the sprite:

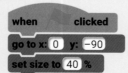

We start the program by clicking the Green flag button. This code will make the runner move to the centre and shrink it to 40% of its size so it fits on the screen.

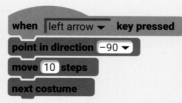

When the left arrow is pressed, the runner will face to the left, then move 10 pixels. It will then change its costume (and show the next frame).

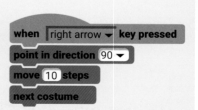

When the right arrow is pressed, the runner will face to the right, then move 10 pixels. It will then change its costume.

 TIP: Press the cursor keys to see your runner move!

14 To stop your runner from rotating when we change direction:

Sprite1

Click the blue **'i'** in the circle for **Sprite1**.

Choose the **arrows**.

Click the **triangle**.

15 Why not add another sprite to make the runner part of a game? We will add code for a game where the runner has to catch as many apples as they can in 30 seconds.

 Click **'Choose sprite from library'**, scroll down and choose **'Apple'**. Click **OK**.

Sprite Library

Apple

16 Drag all this code into the Scripts Area. Make sure you have the **Apple** sprite selected in the Sprites Pane.

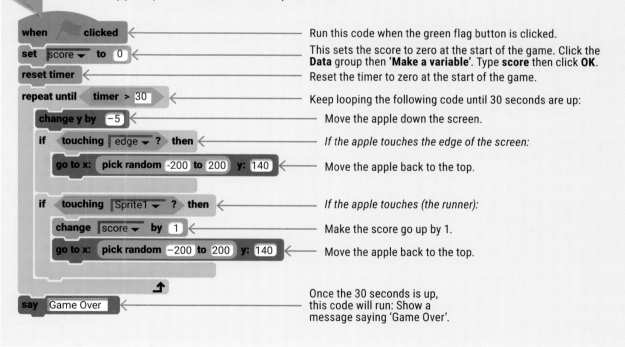

when clicked ← Run this code when the green flag button is clicked.

set score to 0 ← This sets the score to zero at the start of the game. Click the **Data** group then **'Make a variable'**. Type **score** then click **OK**.

reset timer ← Reset the timer to zero at the start of the game.

repeat until timer > 30 ← Keep looping the following code until 30 seconds are up:

change y by -5 ← Move the apple down the screen.

if touching edge ? then ← *If the apple touches the edge of the screen:*

go to x: pick random -200 to 200 y: 140 ← Move the apple back to the top.

if touching Sprite1 ? then ← *If the apple touches (the runner):*

change score by 1 ← Make the score go up by 1.

go to x: pick random -200 to 200 y: 140 ← Move the apple back to the top.

say Game Over ← Once the 30 seconds is up, this code will run: Show a message saying 'Game Over'.

Explore and experiment

Add an exciting animated backdrop to your game. Instead of using a clipart apple, draw your own animated falling object for your runner to catch.

5 DESIGNING IN 3D

In our final chapter, we will look beyond the flat world of the computer screen and into the third dimension. Many games use 3D graphics to give you the impression that you're moving around a virtual world. Designers and architects also use 3D software to plan products and buildings.

What software can I use?

We will be using **SketchUp** to do our 3D design. You can download it for free. Run the part of it called **SketchUp Make**, which is easier to use than the professional version. Turn to page 77 for help with downloading.

After launching SketchUp, click the **Start using SketchUp** button to get going.

To make our drawings look more realistic, we can add perspective. Perspective makes things that are nearer look bigger, and things that are farther away appear to be smaller.

2D versus 3D

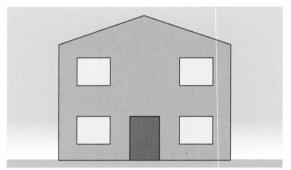

Programs like Microsoft Paint allow us to draw things in 2D. For example, we might draw a house viewed from the front. We can see two of the dimensions: the width and the height.

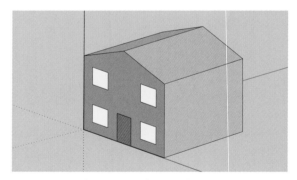

A 3D view of a house shows the depth of the house as well – the third dimension. This view is called isometric.

Tools for drawing in SketchUp

Drawing things in SketchUp is a bit like carving or working with modelling clay. We start with one object, and cut parts out, or stretch bits of it.

Rectangle
We usually start making things with the Rectangle.

Click a start point for the rectangle, then click where you want the opposite corner. Unlike most 2D graphics programs, we don't drag the mouse in SketchUp.

Line
Add lines to an object. The lines become part of the object and can be used to make a roof, for example.

Push/Pull

This makes flat things into thicker 3D things.

Fill
Add colour and textures to your 3D objects.

TIP: Experiment with the camera position using the **Camera** menu. For example, **Camera** then **Standard views** then **Right** will show your artwork from the front.

Try turning off **Perspective** from the same menu by unticking it.

Editing tools

Select
Click one face of an object, or drag a dotted box around a whole object. You can then use the other editing tools.

Scale
Resize an object.

Rotate

Spin an object around.

Move
Move an object or line around.

Undo

Take back any mistakes! (Or click the **Edit** menu and **Undo**.)

Changing the view

In a 3D program, zooming in and out is even more important than in previous chapters. We do this by changing the camera view. To start, or if you can't see everything properly on the screen, click the **Camera** menu then **Standard views** then **Iso** (short for isometric).

Zoom

Click this to move closer or farther out. Drag the magnifying glass cursor up the screen to zoom in, and down to zoom out.

Orbit
Click this tool then drag the mouse around to see from a different angle.

Pan

This moves the view up a bit, or to the left, without rotating.

GET STARTED IN SKETCHUP

To get going with 3D graphics, we're going to start off by learning how to draw a simple cube, or cuboid, like a cardboard box. By having a go at this starter exercise, you'll get to grips with some of SketchUp's key tools and functions.

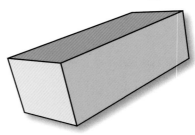

1 Start running **SketchUp**.

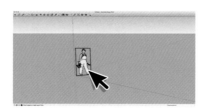

Click the **'Start using SketchUp'** button at the bottom.

2 You'll see some blue sky, the earth (green grass), and a person to give you an idea of size and scale.

We don't need the person, so click her and press the **'Delete'** key.

3 There are various angles from which we can view things in SketchUp. These are controlled by setting the 'camera' position.

One of the simplest views to get started is the isometric view (see page 62). To set this view, click the **Camera** menu, **Standard views** then **Iso**.

Camera		Top
Previous		Bottom
Next		Front
Standard Views	▶	Back
Parallel Projection		Left
✓ Perspective		Right
Two-Point Perspective		**Iso**

4 Now we can start drawing our cube. First, we draw a rectangle for the base.

Click the **Rectangle** button on the SketchUp toolbar:

TIP: If you can't see the **Rectangle** button, look for one of these three shapes instead. Click one then choose **Rectangle** from the menu.

5 Start by clicking where the rectangle will start. **Click** where the three lines on the screen join.

Origin

A yellow circle will appear, and the word **'Origin'**, which means the centre.

6 Now set the opposite corner for the rectangle by clicking to the right.

This rectangle will be the base of our box.

If you make a mistake, click the **Edit** menu then **Undo**.

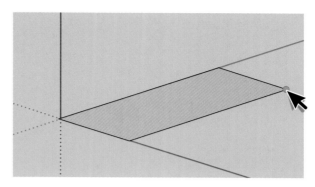

Click here. Don't drag the mouse!

7 Our box is still flat, so we need to make it thicker.

This is a bit like blowing up a balloon – it starts flat but grows thicker. In SketchUp we do this by using the **Push/ Pull** tool. **Click** it.

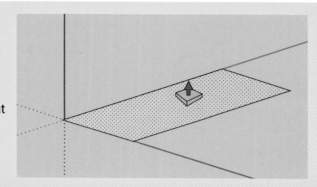

Move your mouse over your rectangle. Lots of dots will appear.

Click it.

Slowly move your mouse up and the box will magically grow.

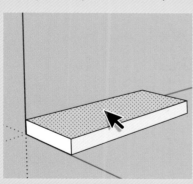
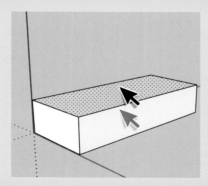
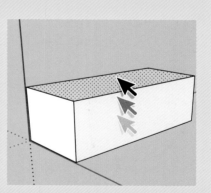

Click again to fix the size of the box.

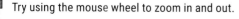

TIP: To view your box at different angles, click the **Orbit** button.

Try using the mouse wheel to zoom in and out.

If you can't see everything properly on the screen, click the **Camera** menu, **Standard views** then **Iso**.

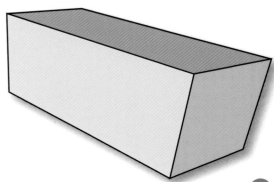

BUILD A HOUSE

Ever wanted to design your own house? Here's your chance! Using SketchUp, we'll design a simple house. Once you are happy with your home, why not add an extension or two?

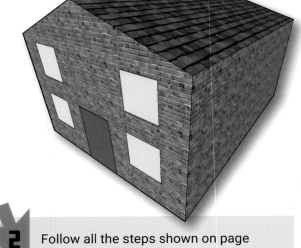

1

Start running **SketchUp**.

Click the **'Start using SketchUp'** button at the bottom.

2

Follow all the steps shown on page 64–5 to make a 3D box, or cuboid.

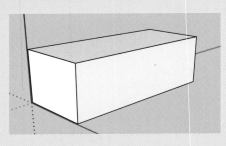

3

This box is a bit long and thin so we need to resize it.

It is made up of a number of lines and sides. We need to select them all.

Click the **Select** tool and draw a selection box around the whole cuboid.

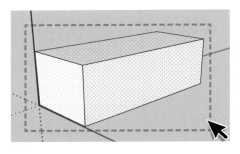

4

Click the **Scale** button.

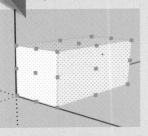
Handles will appear around the box.

Move your mouse over the middle handle at the end.

Slowly **drag** the handle to shrink the box.

Click the mouse button.

5 Now we have finished scaling, click the **Select** button. To make sure nothing is selected, click somewhere green.

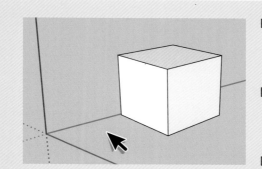

TIP: If you make a mistake click **Edit** then **Undo**.

If you can't see everything properly, click the **Camera** menu then **Standard views** and **Iso**.

6 To make the roof, click on the **Line** tool.

Move your mouse slowly along the top line of the box, until a blue circle appears, showing the midpoint.

Click to start the line from the midpoint.

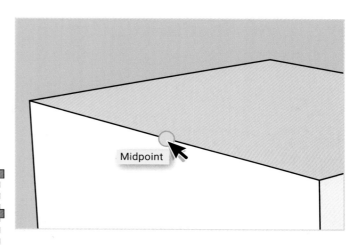

Midpoint

TIP: Because SketchUp is using perspective it may not look in the middle. Remember: perspective means things that are nearer to you appear larger than things that are further away.

7 Move your mouse to the **vertical line at the front**. The end of the line will go red. **Click** to set the line.

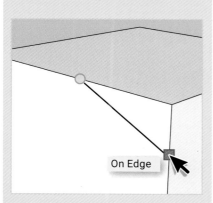

On Edge

8 Move your mouse back to where the line started. A green dot will appear. **Click** to start the second line.

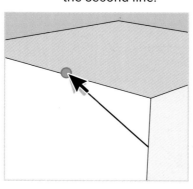

9 Move your mouse to the **vertical line at the back**. The end of the line will turn red.

If you move slowly downward, a green dotted line will show up when the mouse lines up with the end of the first line. **Click** to set the line.

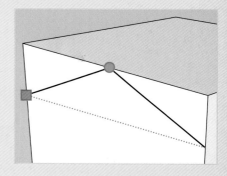

10 We will remove part of the box to make the roof shape.
Click the **Push/Pull** tool.

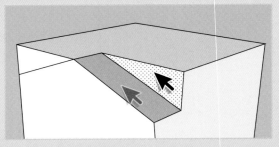

Move your mouse over the triangle at the front. Blue dots will show when it is in the right place.

Click the mouse then move it slowly to the right.

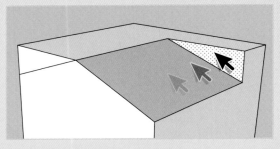

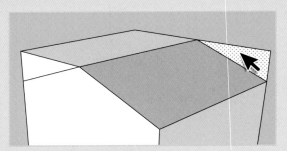

Keep moving your mouse slowly to the right.

Stop when you get to the edge. **Click** the mouse to complete the shape.

11 Repeat step 10 with the other triangle of the roof.

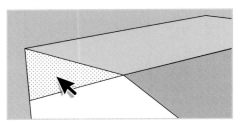

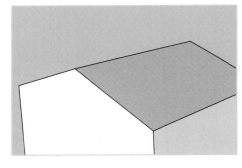

This completes the basic house shape!

12 To add a door, click the **Rectangle** tool.

Move the mouse onto the bottom front line in the middle. A red box will appear.

Click to start the rectangle.

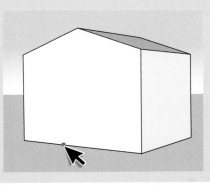

Move the mouse to draw the door shape. **Click** to complete it.

Click the **File** menu then **Save** to save your work.

13 Move the mouse to the right of the door and **click**.

Move up and right to make the window shape. **Click** when you are happy with the size.

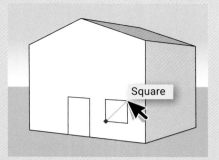

Square

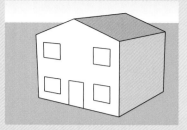

Add more windows in the same way.

14 To colour parts of the house, click the **Fill** tool.

Choose a colour for the door.

Colors

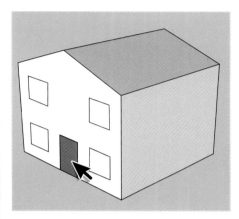

Click the door to colour it. Colour the rest of the house. Use the **Orbit** tool if you need to spin around.

Creating bricks and tiles

Click the brick at the top of the **Colours** palette panel.

Choose a group of textures.

Roofing

Choose a texture.

Click part of your house.

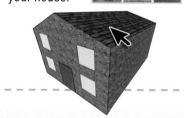

Explore and experiment

When you're happy with your house, why not add an extension:

1 Use the **Line** tool to draw a line from one side of the back of the house to the other.

2 Click the **Push/ Pull** tool and move the mouse over the bottom of the back wall.

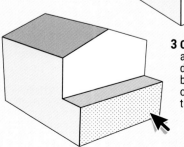

3 Click the wall and slowly drag the bottom half out by moving the mouse.

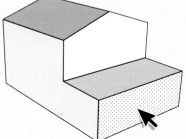

4 Stop moving the mouse when the extension is big enough. **Click** the mouse to fix it.

MODERNIST HOUSE

In the 20th century, modernist architects played around with the forms of their buildings, creating bold and dramatically shaped homes and work spaces. Why not take your inspiration from the work of architects such as Frank Lloyd Wright and Le Corbusier?

1 Start by looking at some examples of modernist architecture. Ask an adult if you can use the Internet, then search for **'modernist architecture'**. Click **'Images'**. Here are some things you might find:

modernist architecture

All **Images** Shopping Videos News More ▾ Search tools

Frank Lloyd Wright
Hollyhock House,
USA, 1921

William Lescaze
High Cross House,
England, 1932

Le Corbusier
Heidi Weber Museum,
Switzerland, 1967

2 Use the **Rectangle** tool to draw a rectangle.

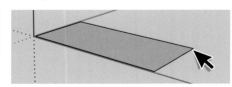

3 Use the **Push/Pull** tool to make it higher.

4 Now we will draw a rectangle on top of the building to make one section of it higher.

Click the **Rectangle** tool.

Move your mouse to the corner of the block. A green circle will appear. **Click**.

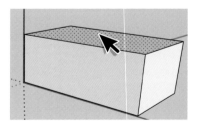

Next move your mouse to a point on the other edge of the building. A red circle will appear. **Click**.

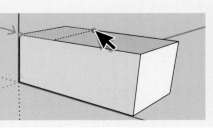

5 Use the **Push/Pull** tool to make the rectangle stand higher. This could be a roof garden!

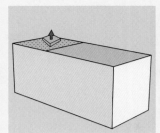

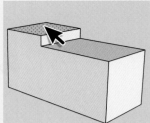

6 Use the **Rectangle** tool to draw lots of large windows. Use the **Orbit** tool to move around.

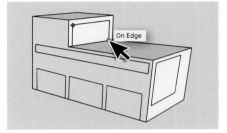

On Edge

7 Click the **Fill** tool and choose a colour.

On the **Colours** palette panel, set the **Opacity** to **25%**.

Opacity   25 %

8 **Click** a window to make it transparent. Look inside!

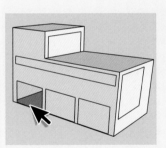

9 **Fill** all your windows, using the **Orbit** tool to move around. The basic house is now complete.

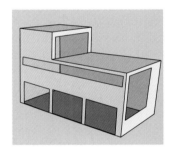

Explore and experiment

With modernist buildings, a lot of thought goes into details and finishes such as cladding.

Be inspired and start experimenting:

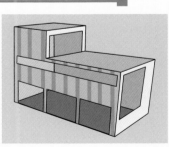

Clad some of the walls in wood, or other textures. Turn to page 69 for help with this.

Turn to page 69 for help with this.

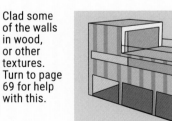

Use the **Rectangle** tool to add some balustrades to stop anyone falling off the roof.

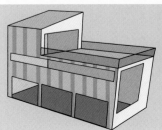

Use the **Fill** tool to turn the balustrades into glass.

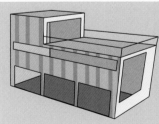

Change the shape further with the **Push/Pull** and **Move** tools.

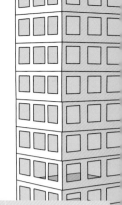

SKYSCRAPER

In crowded modern cities, many people live and work in skyscrapers because they occupy less land. We are going to design our own skyscraper using SketchUp. Then, why not build a whole business district?

1 Start by drawing a square on the ground with the **Rectangle** tool.

First **click** where the lines join, the **'origin'**.

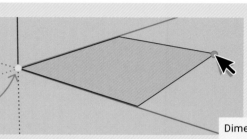

Then **click** on the opposite side of the square to set it.

The dimensions (size) of the square are shown in the bottom right corner as you draw it.

| Dimensions | 4.00m, 4.00m |

2 Now we need to turn the square into the ground floor of the building. Click the **Push/Pull** tool.

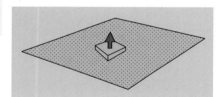

Click the square in the middle. Move the mouse up then **click again** when it is thick enough.

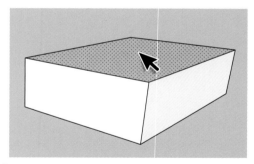

3 To draw windows, choose the **Rectangle** tool.

Move the mouse to the right position and **click**.

Move up and right to make the window shape. **Click** when you are happy with the size.

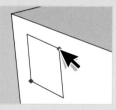

Add more windows.

Make sure you add windows on all four sides, using the **Orbit** tool to spin around.

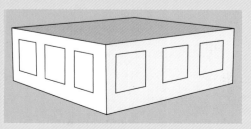

4 To make your windows look like glass, click the **Fill** tool and choose a colour.

On the **Colours** palette panel set the **Opacity** to **25%**.

Opacity

| 25 | % |

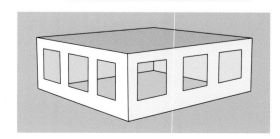

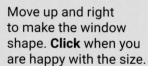

5 We will now add duplicates of the ground floor to make the building. Click the **Select** tool.

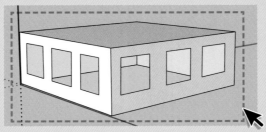

Drag a selection box around the whole of the ground floor.

Click **Edit** then **Copy**.

Edit
Undo
Redo
Cut
Copy
Paste

6 Click **Edit** then **Paste**.

To do your pasting effectively, you will probably need to zoom out. Click the **Zoom** tool, then drag it down the screen.

Drag the new floor into place.

Click **Edit** then **Paste**.

Drag the new floor into place.

7 Keep adding floors until your building is complete.

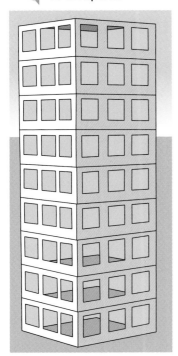

Make sure you save your skyscraper. You will need it later!

Explore and experiment

Why not try making a tower or monument?

1 Start with a tall thin box. (You will need to zoom out and use the **Pan** tool to move around.)

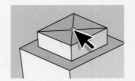

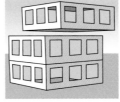

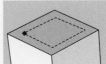

2 Draw another rectangle on top, and use the **Push/Pull** tool to lift it slightly.

3 Use the **Line** tool to draw diagonals carefully on top.

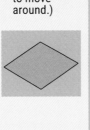

4 Choose the **Move** tool. **Click** the point where the diagonal lines join.

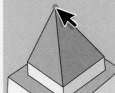

5 Slowly pull up the top of the tower. **Click** to set the height. Add any other ideas of your own!

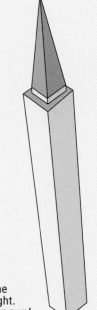

CREATE A CITY

Now we have learnt how to make different building types, we can combine them into a city. We'll start by making roads, then copy and paste houses, buildings and monuments. You need to have made the previous activities and saved them before you start this activity!

1 Start running **SketchUp**.

We don't need the person, so click her and press the '**Delete**' key.

2 Draw a main road to start the city off. Click the **Rectangle** tool and draw a long thin rectangle.

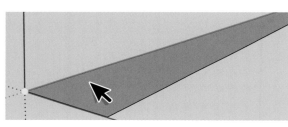

You may find it easier to type in the dimensions of the road. First click the start point, and move the mouse to start the rectangle. Now just type **5500** and press '**Enter**'.

Dimensions | 5,500

3 Use the **Rectangle** tool to add more roads joining the main one.

The red square will appear when a new rectangle joins the main road.

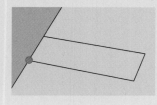

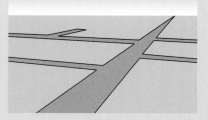

If you make a mistake click the **Edit** menu then **Undo**.

If you can't see everything on the screen, click **Camera** then **Standard views** and **Iso**.

Don't be afraid to start again if everything goes wrong. The more you practise with any software, the easier it will get.

Save your work as '**City**'.

4 Now we will add buildings. Click the **File** menu, then **Open**. Find some of the buildings you saved.

New
Open
Open recent ▶

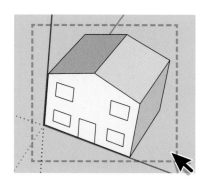

Click the **Select** tool. Drag a dotted select box around the whole building.

Click the **Edit** menu then **Copy**.

Undo
Redo
Cut
Copy
Paste

5 Next we need to bring the copy of your house into the city. You should have two windows open in SketchUp, the city and the house.

Click the **Window** menu and look at the bottom of all the options.

Window

| Photo Textures |
| Bring All to Front |
| **City – SketchUp** |
| House – SketchUp |

Click on **'City'** to go back to your city 3D model.

6 Click **Edit** and **Paste**. Move the mouse away from the menu to see your house.

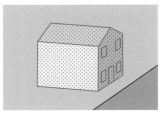

Move the house next to a road and **click** to place it.

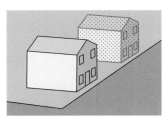

Paste more houses on to the city by clicking **Edit** and **Paste**.

7 To add other buildings, go back to step 4 and open another of your saved files. Follow steps 5 and 6 to add them.

8 Add things, like paths and fences, around houses using the **Rectangle** tool.

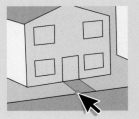

Rotating buildings

1 If you need to rotate a building, use the **Select** tool to select the whole building.

2 Click the **Rotate** tool.

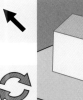
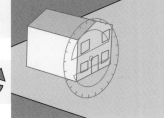

3 Move the mouse slowly around the building until the protractor turns blue. This shows that the building will rotate on the ground.

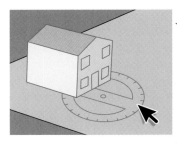

4 **Click** to set the way it will rotate (on the ground), then **click again** to set the point it rotates around.

5 Now slowly move your mouse to rotate the house.

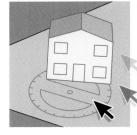

6 **Click** to set it in place.

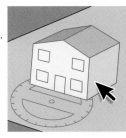

 To view your city from different angles, click the **Orbit** button.

ADVICE ON SOFTWARE

Always check you are downloading the software you are looking for. Sometimes there will be adverts on a web page that take you to other downloads, some of which may be 'malware': programs that can harm your computer or contain viruses. Always ask permission from the person who owns the computer before downloading any software. Neither the author nor the publisher can be held responsible for the content of software downloaded from websites referred to in this book. For more information on the software used in this book visit: www.ictapps.com/20.

Vector graphics with OpenOffice

You can download a free copy of **Apache OpenOffice** for a Windows PC, Mac or Linux computer. Make sure you go to the official website. Follow these instructions:

1   Go to **www.openoffice.org**.

 I want to download Apache OpenOffice

2   Click the green arrow.
3   Follow the steps on screen to install the software.
4   You will get a choice of whether to install the **Complete** OpenOffice Suite (all the programs) or to do a **Custom** installation. The custom option will let you choose the vector graphics program **Draw** on its own.

Bitmap software on Windows

Every Windows PC or laptop should have a copy of **Microsoft Paint**. On older PCs, there should be a link to Microsoft Paint in the Accessories group (click **Start** > **Programs** > **Accessories** > **Paint**). On Windows 10, click the Windows **Start** button, then type **'paint'** into the white box. Press the **'Enter'** key.

On older Windows computers, some of the icons and tools may be in different places. If you cannot see a Copy or Paste button on the tool bar, click **Edit > Copy** or **Edit > Paste**. If there is no zoom slider, you can use the magnifier icon next to the shape tools.

Bitmap software on a Mac

There is no graphics editor like Microsoft Paint included on a Mac. For younger children, **TuxPaint** is free and will allow you to draw simple pictures. It can be downloaded from **www.tuxpaint.org**. The first few activities in the book can be completed with this software. The graphics editor in **Scratch** (see opposite) could also be used for simple tasks.

To complete the more advanced activities, more powerful software is needed. **Paint X Lite** can be downloaded from iTunes. The Lite version of the software is free and works in a very similar way to Microsoft Paint. Search for **'paint x lite itunes'** in your browser. Go to **iTunes** and follow the instructions to download the software. Note: to zoom, you will need to use the **View** tab or menu.

For older or more experienced children, **Photoshop** and the other photo-editing software suggested opposite could be an alternative.

Photo-editing software

If you have a Windows PC or laptop, you will be able to use **Microsoft Paint** for all the photo-editing activities in this book. See 'Bitmap software on Windows' opposite for advice on finding and using it. **Paint.net** is a good free alternative, but only for Windows.

If you have a Mac, a free photo-editing program is **Paint X Lite**. See 'Bitmap software on a Mac' opposite for advice on downloading and using it. With Paint X Lite, you will be able to carry out all the photo-editing activities in this book, apart from 'Pop Art poster' on pages 46–9, and 'Digital graffiti' on pages 50–51. This is because Paint X Lite does not allow you to save as 16- or 2-colour bitmaps. **Pixlr** is another free alternative for Macs. You can use it online at **https:/pixlr.com/editor**. It is possible to upload and copy images but because it is running online this can be more fiddly than using a program that runs on your computer.

Alternatively, you can purchase a program like **Photoshop**, **PaintShop Pro** or **Photoshop Elements**, which is a simpler version of **Photoshop**. These will allow you to carry out all the activities in this book, but remember: you don't need to purchase one of these programs to improve your photo-editing skills. Bear in mind that different programs use different icons, menus and buttons to carry out the same task, and that different versions of a piece of software will change. We recommend that, if possible, you try software before buying so you can ensure it does what you want and your children can use it effectively. You can purchase Adobe Photoshop or Photoshop Elements from **www.adobe.com/uk**. Check out the discounts for students and teachers. There is also a free trial option so you can get a feel for the software before purchasing, as it is expensive.

Animation with Scratch

You can use **Scratch** on a PC or Mac by opening your web browser and going to: **http://scratch.mit.edu**. Then click **Try it out**.

If you want to run Scratch without using the internet, you can download it here: **http://scratch.mit.edu/scratch2download/**.

There is a very similar website called **Snap** that also works on iPads. It is available here: **http://snap.berkeley.edu/run**.

3D graphics with SketchUp

You can download a free copy of **SketchUp** if you are a student and are going to use it only for educational purposes. If you become an architect and start selling your designs, you will need to buy a full licence! You can use SketchUp on a Mac or on a Windows PC. Follow these instructions:

1   Go to **www.sketchup.com**.

2   Click **Download SketchUp**.
3   Ask an adult if you can fill in the form and download the software. You need to make sure you choose these options:
   You are going to use the software for Educational Use.
   Choose 'SketchUp Make'.
4   Follow the steps on screen to install the software.

GOING FURTHER WITH PHOTOS

Working with photos is both exciting and tricky. Here is a bit more advice on difficult techniques such as downloading, uploading and resizing. Plus, we've got some extra help for Mac users and anyone who wants to take their photo-editing to the next level!

Using your own images

Using your own digital photographs with the techniques covered in this book can make for amazing and original results. It can sometimes be tricky to upload your photos from a phone or camera. There are many different systems available to do this, but your computer should be able to handle one of these methods:

Cloud syncing

This is the simplest way to get images from a camera or phone to a computer. You will need to check with your device how to set this up. It means that every time a photo is taken on the device it automatically gets uploaded to a 'cloud' (an online storage area). This is then 'synced' (synchronized with your computer's photo storage area).

Memory card

If you have a digital camera it will probably have a memory card to store photographs on. This is usually called an SD card. Once you have taken photos, remove this card and put it into your computer. If your computer doesn't have a slot, it may have a special box on a USB cable that you can plug the SD card into. The SD card should show up in **Finder** (on a Mac) or **Explorer** (in Windows).

USB cable

Most cameras, tablets and phones come with a cable that allows them to be plugged into a computer. Once plugged in, a program should start up to help you import new images. You may need to search for information about your device to find out if you need special software to do this. The program should allow you to **Open** or **Copy** the images.

Bluetooth

Some cameras and phones will have a bluetooth connection which will allow you to send images to a nearby computer. New images will probably be sent to the **Downloads** area. This technology is called **AirDrop** on Apple devices.

Email or social media

An alternative is to view an image on a phone then use the **Send** icon to email it to yourself. You can then open your email on a computer and **Download** the image. It is also possible to do this with various social media tools – but remember that other people may be able to see your photos.

Using images from the web

It is easy to search for images on the web, but you must ask permission from an adult first. Whether you can use a photo or not depends on what kind of copyright the person who took the photo has decided to give it. If you are just using the image to try out something at home or for a school project, it may well be OK to use it whatever its copyright – that depends on the laws of the country you live in. An alternative is to search for images that are **'free to use, share or modify'**:

1   Go to **www.google.com**.

3   Click **Options** then **Advanced search**.

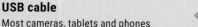

- Search settings
- Languages
- **Advanced search**
- History
- Search help

2   Search for something. Click **images**.

dinosaur

4   Find **Usage rights** then choose **Free to use, share or modify**. Click **Advanced search**.

usage rights   free to use, share or modify ▾

Advanced Search

Image size

When working with digital images, they can often be too big or too small.

Too big: You will see only part of the image in Microsoft Paint or other photo-editing software. It will also take up lots of storage space and may make your program run slowly.

Solution: Resize the photo. For instructions on resizing in Microsoft Paint, see page 35.

Too small: The image may either be small on the page, or probably be pixelated (it will look very 'blocky').

Solution: You need to download a higher-resolution version of the image, or retake the photo at a higher resolution setting (with a higher MP, or mega pixel, setting).

Just right!

Avoiding pixelation with web images: If you are using a picture from the web don't copy it from the results page.

Click through to a larger version (find **View image**) of the image before copying it.

Cropping images

When photographs contain more things than you want, or are the wrong shape, you need to crop them.

Resizing the image to make it square will just distort it and look strange!

Cropping the image allows you to choose the shape and size, while keeping the proportions.

Look for the **Crop** icon, or use the **Select** tool, then **Copy** part of the image.

For Mac users and more

If you're using Photoshop, Photoshop Elements, Paint.net or PaintShop Pro, here are some tools you will find useful. These programs also include special brushes, filters to change the colour of a picture, brightness and contrast controls, and many other features to take your work to the next level.

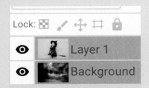

Layers

Instead of using separate copies of Microsoft Paint, you use different 'layers' to store the background and the photo you are adding. Click on the layer you want to edit in the **Layer** window.

Magic wand tool

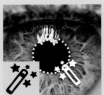

The **Magic wand** tool allows you to select a large area in one click. It is a quick way to remove part of the background of a photo. It works by selecting all the pixels that are a similar shade.

Free rotation

Microsoft Paint only allows rotation 90 degrees at a time. In Photoshop, select an area, **right-click** (on a Mac, hold '**Ctrl**' and click) then choose **Free transform**. Move your mouse below the handles and drag to rotate to any angle.

Opacity

Choose a brush to paint with, then set its **Opacity**. 20% means the paint will be almost transparent. Higher numbers make the paint more opaque.

Clone tool

Select part of a photo to clone, or copy (such as sky or trees), then brush across part of the photo you want to lose (such as a building) to see it disappear!

Glossary

Animation A series of pictures that are shown one after the other to give the illusion of movement.

Bitmap A grid of tiny squares (or pixels) used to make up an image.

BMP The file type used to store a bitmap on a computer as a grid of pixels.

CMYK A format used to store colour information for printing. C = Cyan, M = Magenta, Y = Yellow, K = Key (black).

Code A series of instructions or commands.

Command A word or code block that tells the computer what to do.

Copy and paste A method of duplicating objects or part of an image by creating a copy of it and 'sticking' it down in a new place.

Dimensions The size – width, height (and thickness) – of an object.

Drawing Area The right-hand part of the screen in Scratch that is used to draw sprites and backgrounds.

Flip Change part of an image so that it looks as though it has been reflected horizontally (left-right) or vertically (up-down).

Handle A small button in a graphics program that allows an object or part of an image to be stretched to make it larger or smaller.

Isometric A way of showing 3D objects on a screen or paper.

JPG A file type often used to store photos on computers. It is similar to a BMP file but takes up less space by ignoring small details within the picture.

Opacity The opposite of transparency. An object with 100% opacity cannot be seen through.

Palette The colours available to use in a graphics program.

Perspective A technique used in 3D graphics to make things look more realistic. Objects that are farther away are drawn smaller.

Pixel A tiny dot on a computer screen, combined with thousands of other pixels to make up an image.

PNG A file type used to store a bitmap. Unlike the BMP format, it compresses the file to make it smaller by looking for areas of the same colour.

Program Set of instructions that allows a computer to perform tasks.

Scratch A computer language that uses blocks of code to make a program.

Scripts Area The area to the right of the Scratch screen where code blocks are dragged to create programs.

Selection Choosing part of an image before changing or moving it.

Software A program used by a computer.

Sprite An object or character that can be commanded to move around the screen.

3D graphics A way of drawing objects with three dimensions – height, width and depth – on a computer screen.

Transparency An object, or part of an image, that we can see through.

Vector graphics A system used to store a picture made up of different shapes or objects. Each one is stored as information including coordinates, colour, size and line thickness.

Zoom Moving in to show a close-up of a computer graphics image.

Index